Canyon Country
Paddles

A practical, informative, and entertaining
guide to river running using the kayak,
canoe, or rubber raft in southeastern Utah.

By
Verne Huser

1978
Wasatch Publishers, Inc.

This mini-book is number TWELVE in a series of practical guides to travel and recreation in the scenic Colorado Plateau region of the Four Corners states

All written material, maps, and photographs by Verne Huser unless otherwise credited

COVER: Canoeing on the Green River.

Copyright © 1978
Wasatch Publishers, Inc.
4647 Idlewild Road
Salt Lake City, Utah 84117
All rights reserved
ISBN 0-915272-18-0

Dedicated to Maki, who helped me run the rivers, and to Willa, who helped us both.

ACKNOWLEDGEMENTS: Don Baars, Fran Barnes, Bill Belknap, Dave Conley, Kim Crumbo, Jay Dewell, A.C. Ekker, Duane Erickson, Cal Giddings, Ray Grass, Dee and Sue Holladay, Jim Isenogle, Ken Ross, Ken Sleight, Gay Staveley, Reece Stein, Russell Sullivan, Tedd Tuttle, Ray Varley, Howard Valle, John Williams, Ann Zwinger and others.

Contents

Introduction 7
    Region Covered 8
    General Terrain 9
    River Administration 10
    Antiquities Laws 11
    Seasonal Variations 12
    A Parting Shot 13
    Note On General River Running 14

Crafts and Equipment 15
    Inflatables 16
    Hard-Hulled Boats 17
    Canoes 18
    Kayaks 19
    Dories 19
    Sportyak 19
    Equipment 21

Logistics 27
    Transportation 27
    Area Map 28
    Food and Water 30
    Cooking and Camping 30
    River Etiquette 32

Health and Safety 35

Natural Information 41
    Vegetation.. 41
    Animals 43
    Birds... 45
    Geology 48
    History... 49

The Colorado River............................. 53

The Green River 63

The San Juan River 71

Seasonal Rivers................................. 81
    Muddy Creek 82
    The Dolores River 84
    The Escalante River 87
    The Dirty Devil 89

Bibliography..................................... 91

Photo courtesy American River Touring Assn.

Introduction

Much of southeastern Utah, the scope of this book, is wilderness by its very nature, wild rugged country that almost defies access. The pioneer spirit prevails among the people of the area and in many there exists an antipathy to the natural wilderness and an insatiable desire to conquer it.

Man has built roads into the area, and off-road vehicles have pushed back the wilderness boundaries in the name of mineral exploration, drilling activities for gas and oil, and recreation. Much of the canyon country, however, still remains inaccessible except by river, the natural routes of this standing-up country.

Many of the main roads follow rivers or courses cut by rivers in the past. Most of the off-road vehicle trails use stream beds for part of their course across this colorful country. River routes can frequently be followed, at least in part, on foot or on horseback, but in many places roads and trails stop at the canyon rim hundreds of feet above the river. While most rivers are accessible in many places by road or trail, certain stretches can be reached only by the rivers that carved this magnificent land.

Auto access to the rivers is vital to those who would float the waters of the area because they need launch and landing sites and re-supply points on extended trips. Without going into great detail, this guidebook will mention the major access points, some of which can only be reached by off-road vehicle (Four Wheel Drive).

Limited access becomes a safety factor that needs careful consideration. If you have an accident or someone gets sick or your craft is damaged, how will you find help or reach safety? Don't try running a Canyon Country river until you have worked out all the logistic details. There is enough risk involved in running rivers not to leave anything to chance if you can control it.

Careful planning is vital: transportation, food and water, knowledge of the region and general terrain as well as river running skills and knowledge of the specific river or river segment, some understanding of flow fluctuations, administrative edicts, river etiquette, weather patterns, antiquities laws, and human nature. Some of this knowledge you can get from reading (see Bibliography at the end of the book), but for the most part it comes through experience, practical knowledge that you gain only by doing.

Outdoor experience gained through camping and hiking is valuable and has a great deal of carry-over value for running rivers, but there are certain skills—like reading water—that come only from experience on the river. That experience should not be gained by accident—though you can learn a great deal from accidents. Use common sense and go with someone who is familiar with river running before you try it on your own, a commercial guide perhaps or a friend, neighbor, or relative who knows something about boating on moving water.

River running can be safe, fun and highly rewarding if it is done properly with careful planning and complete follow-through on every detail. It can also be disastrous. Only you can make the difference between a positive experience and a negative one. Accidents don't just happen; they are precipitated by poor planning and inexperience. Gain your experience carefully.

REGION COVERED: This guidebook will cover the major rivers and several minor (seasonal) streams in the region south of I-70 within the immediate Colorado River drainage in Utah and far western Colorado. It is roughly the southeastern quarter of Utah, the area covered by Multipurpose Maps 1 (Southeastern Utah) and 2 (Southeastern Central Utah), which are widely available from state and federal agency offices and numerous private distributors at a nominal fee.

Each river will be dealt with in some detail, and specific maps will be suggested for each. The best river map for much

Canoeists prepare for run down Labyrinth Canyon

of the area is Bill and Buzz Belknap's *Canyonlands River Guide* published by Westwater Books (Box 365, Boulder City, NV 89005). It covers all of the Colorado and Green rivers in the area as well as Lake Powell.

Western Colorado is included because the launch area for two major runs through Utah waters on the Colorado and Dolores rivers respectively lie in western Colorado. Since rivers do not alter when they cross a stateline, I have also included all of the popular run on the Dolores in Colorado. Both segments — the Colorado and the Dolores — are under consideration for Wild and Scenic Rivers System protection.

GENERAL TERRAIN: The rivers covered by this guidebook all flow through the Colorado Plateau, most of which is considered high desert though some massive peaks lie in the surrounding countryside. However, the rivers have carved deep canyons through the ancient sedimentary rocks of the region. It is a badly broken country of confusing contour. It is hard to get lost on the river, for the current flows forever downstream, but if you do much sidecanyon hiking — and that is at least half of the pleasure of the trip — you can get lost or rimmed-out or trapped by flash floods that may roar down dry arroyos from sudden showers miles away.

It is a dry land, a rocky land, a vertical land. It is a land of livestock grazing and four-wheel-drive vehicles, of miners and drillers, of Indian ruins and rock art—all dictated by the geology of the area and by the availability or lack of water, by the lay of the land. Listen to the names: Labyrinth Canyon, the Maze, the Loop; Hardscrabble Bottom, Upheaval Dome, Ragged Mountain; Sinbad Country.

Of course, all those names aren't necessarily river-bottom tags, but they describe the general terrain. On some river trips the shuttle (ferrying cars from launch to landing) may be as spectacular as the scene from the river, and to see the country from river level and from above can be doubly fulfilling.

RIVER ADMINISTRATION: All of the rivers in Canyon Country fall into several jurisdictions: federal, state, and local. Each may have its own rules and regulations, but for the most part they are synchronized. Coast Guard-approved personal flotation devices (PFD's) must be carried (federal law) and worn (state law) while people are on the river.

An up-dated list of current laws and regulations relating to river running in Utah may be obtained from the Utah Division of Parks and Recreation, 1596 West North Temple, Salt Lake City, Utah 84116. They dove-tail with federal laws and regulations in most instances. At present the person in charge of any passenger-for-hire river trip must arrange for at least one person on the trip to have a current Red Cross standard first aid card or equivalent.

It is not a bad idea for private trips to follow the same regulations required of commercial operators. All parties—private and public—are required by state law to obtain a permit from the Bureau of Land Management before embarking on river trips on the Colorado River in Westwater Canyon, the Dolores River in Utah, and the San Juan River above Mexican Hat and from the National Park Service for running river trips on the lower San Juan in Glen Canyon National Recreation Area and the Colorado River through Cataract Canyon in Canyonlands National Park.

Addresses for National Park Service offices are as follows: Utah State Office, National Park Service, 125 South State Street, Salt Lake City, UT 84111; Canyonlands National Park, (for Cataract Canyon) 446 South Main, Moab, UT 84532; Glen Canyon National Recreation Area, (for the lower San

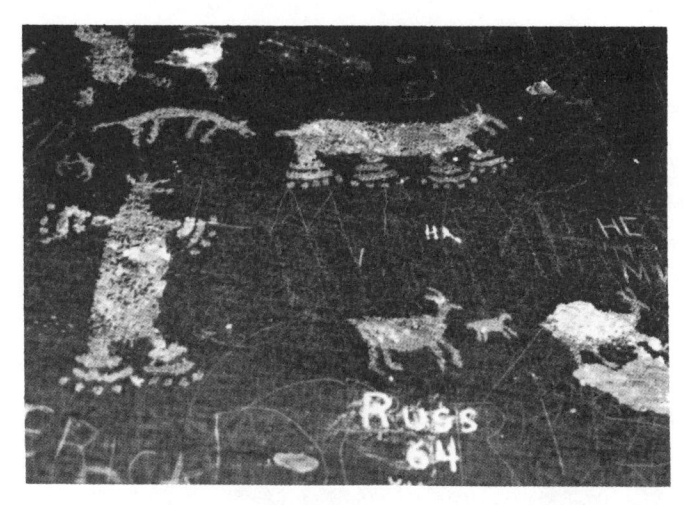

Petroglyphs - ancient and more recent

Juan) Box 1507, Page, AZ 86040. Addresses for the Bureau of Land Management are as follows: Utah State Office, Bureau of Land Management, 136 East South Temple, Salt Lake City, UT 84111; Grand Resource Area, 446 South Main, Moab, UT 84532 (Westwater and Dolores); San Juan Resource Area, Box 1327, Monticello, UT 84535 (San Juan River).

ANTIQUITIES LAWS: Simply stated, it is illegal and inappropriate to remove from the public lands any artifacts, fossils, or relics of the past that might be of scientific interest. It is illegal and stupid to damage any structure or work of art, Indian or historic site or petroglyph or pictograph.

Canyon Country is rich in pre-historic Indian ruins and conrete evidence of earlier man. Some of it has not yet been discovered — new finds come to light nearly every year. While it may be true that more sites have been lost to Lake Powell than are left, abundant evidence remains in the Canyon Country, most of it along the river corridors, and it should be protected.

This guidebook will not pinpoint any sites not already well known. Please take good care of the sites you visit, the ruins you find. Do not loot them or vandalize their contents. Report them to proper authorities and help protect them. Anything you remove from a site will not be there for others to enjoy. You are stealing from the public treasury when you take for your own what belongs to everyone and to the ages. Indians on the reservation sometimes deal harshly with violators of their ancient sites — everything south of the San Juan is Navajo Reservation.

State and federal laws protect the antiquities, but only you can provide the enforcement of such laws through responsible action on the site. Take nothing but pictures; leave nothing but footprints.

SEASONAL VARIATIONS: River running is a seasonal activity depending upon adequate flows of water in the streams and comfortable temperatures. Spring is the best season for running most of the rivers in Canyon Country because water levels are high, vegetation is green, potable water is more readily available, the birds are more abundant, the heat of summer has not yet descended upon the area, and the masses of people have not yet come.

Most of the minor (seasonal) streams are runnable only for a brief period during the spring when snow melt and spring rains coincide. In dry years, they may not be runnable at all. The big rapids are bigger during the snow-melt run-off, and the sand waves on the San Juan are at their best when reservoir-release flows are augmented by natural run-off.

Summer is hot along the rivers of Canyon Country, but in early summer the rivers may still be high since in most cases their headwaters are high in the mountains many miles upstream. More services are available during the summer, and what wildflowers don't bloom in the spring blossom during the heat of July and August. The weather is more certain, and the mosquitoes may have subsided, but potable water is less certain. Nights are often pleasantly cool along the rivers in the high desert. Flash floods occur during thunderstorm activity, and despite the heat, more people run the rivers.

Autumn may be the best time for photography. River-side vegetation turns yellow and skies seem to clear. Nights get cool and in the later autumn, days do too. Beaver become more active and river runners less active as the tourist season passes. Indian summer is late, long and lovely in the canyons of the Green and Colorado and San Juan. Storms may come occasionally, but they normally don't last long. They may leave snow at higher elevations, creating picturesque back

San Juan River launch area at Mexican Hat

drops. Rivers are low, and you will have to carry water, but you won't need as much because temperatures are lower. Fall is my favorite time to run the rivers of Canyon Country.

Don't count out winter for river running, especially for short runs. Warm sunny days occur often between winter storms, and while overnight temperatures may be low and canyon shadows cool, you can get in some good runs during the winter months. Go prepared if you do run the rivers this time of year: wear wet suits—the water is cold—and take along plenty of dry wool clothing, and don't get wet.

Canyon Country offers year 'round river running for the hardy.

A PARTING SHOT: People run rivers for many reasons. Some seek the thrill of running rapids; they exist in Canyon Country, but you have to pick your segments and seasons. Some seek the ancient Indian ruins, relics and rock art; there is no better place on earth than the canyons of the San Juan, Green and Colorado, but you will have to do some off river hiking to find the best.

Some seek solitude; there is solitude aplenty in the canyons of southeastern Utah's rivers, especially in the off season—before Memorial Day or after Labor Day. If you seek solitude, don't run the Green or Colorado over Memorial Day weekend because that's when the power boaters run down the Green and up the Colorado on the annual Friendship Cruise. The river is crowded then and noisy, not a proper place for solitude.

On the other hand, if you seek companionship and festivity, try the Friendship Cruise. Memorial Day Weekend officially opens the season on the Green and Colorado rivers though many river runners have been taking trips for weeks by then—I have canoed the Green through Labyrinth Canyon in early April, and that wasn't too early.

Perhaps you want to see wildlife. Birding is especially good on the rivers, at its best in during the spring. If you fish, you will find plenty of opportunity drifting slowly along most Canyon Country rivers. Hunting by boat is popular in Westwater Canyon and a few other stretches, but know your rules and regulations and your area.

River running is not dangerous if you know what you are doing, and in Utah there are many ways to learn: going with a commercial outfitter or a knowledgeable friend or relative, taking a university class in canoeing or kayaking, going with a club or organization. It can be great family fun, but be careful and take good care of the rivers.

NOTE ON GENERAL RIVER RUNNING: This guidebook does not pretend to teach anyone how to run a river. No book can do that. However, a number of how-to books on river running have appeared since 1975, when my own *River Running* was published, the first of its kind, to help lay the groundwork for learning to run rivers.

The present guidebook is not one of them. Rather, it is a guide to a region, Canyon Country, the southeastern corner of Utah, a region of fabulous rivers: the Colorado, the Green, the San Juan, and a number of seasonal streams that offer unique boating possibilities.

Crafts and Equipment

Any number of different kinds of crafts can be used on the rivers of southeastern Utah, some more successfully than others. Keeping in mind that most of the runable rivers in the area have either rocky rapids and riffles or shallow sand bars much of the year, whatever craft you choose should have a shallow draft, the shallower the better in most cases.

Certainly you will be looking for stability if you plan to run any of the rougher water — Cataract Canyon, Westwater Canyon). Carrying capacity may be another consideration, especially if you plan extended or overnight trips with your family. You will probably have to carry along camping gear unless you plan to car camp from the river with a shuttle car joining you at accessible campsites, which is a possibility for some runs. Maneuverability, especially on the rocky rivers, will be still another factor to consider in selecting your craft.

Will you have to portage it? It had better be lightweight. How will you haul it to the river? A car-top carrier can be used for the canoe or kayak but will not do for a dory. Inflatables take up little room, can be conveniently carried in the trunk of a car. What kind of water do you plan to run? Certainly you won't use an open canoe in Cataract Canyon, but decked canoes might be fun for experts. The kind of trip you want to run, the kind of water you expect to run the basic purpose of your trip will all dictate the kind of craft you use.

INFLATABLES: Inflatable crafts have become popular since World War II though few of them were used before the war. Today boats made especially for river running range from individual canoe or kayak types through small rafts—which really aren't rafts—to huge pontoons. The only real rafts are composites made up of several—usually three to five—single inflated tubes or bladders fastened together like logs to form a raft of sorts. They may be lashed or chained or snap-linked together to create a broad sturdy craft. Usually some kind of platform is added on which gear is packed and to which a motormount or rowing frame is attached. Such composite crafts, often called J-rigs for Jack Currey, who invented them, are frequently powered by motor since they are normally large and heavy. J-rigs have great stability and carrying capacity, but they are expensive and too much of a freight barge for many river runners who prefer smaller crafts.

Most of the river running in Canyon Country is done in small rubber boats: several Campway models like the Havasu, Shoshone, Miwok and Apache; several of the Avon boats like the Redshank, Adventurer, Professional or Spirit; or modern Rubber Crafter models of the Yampa and Green. For Campway products write to Campways, Inc., 12915 South Spring Street, Los Angeles, CA 90061 or see Walton Marine in Salt Lake City (3031 South 500 East). For Avon boats contact Seagull Marine, 1851 McGaw Avenue, Irvine, CA 92705. For Rubber Crafter's products, contact Dave Demaree, Box 8, Ohiopyle, PA 15470 or Rubber Crafters, Inc., Box 207, Grantsville, WV 26147.

In big-water rapids like Cataract Canyon small boats are often lashed together, side-by-side, to form what is commonly called a G-rig for Georgie White, the woman who invented this kind of arrangement for floating the once-mighty waters of the Colorado River in Grand Canyon. a G-rig can be run with a motor or with oars and provides good stability in big water.

Manufacturers have developed numerous small individual inflatable crafts during the past two decades from Water-walkers for fishermen and super-light back-packer rafts to inflatable kayaks. Rick Kremmer's *A Guide to Paddle Adventure* (Vanguard 1975) has a good chapter on these mini-boats, many of which are little more than toys though I have seen them used in Grand Canyon and on the Rogue and Salmon rivers. Few of them have more than a single air chamber,

A small rubber raft - Photo courtesy Ray Grass

however, and if that is punctured, you may have to walk home. It pays to find a sturdy craft with more than a single air chamber, but the inexpensive crafts can be good learning boats.

HARD-HULLED BOATS: Hard-hulled boats include canoes and kayaks, dories and sportyaks and a variety of other vessels including aluminum row-boats and jetboats. Motors can be a problem on the shallow rivers and in rocky rapids, but they do provide more range and certain access advantages, and they can be mighty helpful when your float trip ends on the dead-water of a reservoir like Lake Powell.

The annual Friendship Cruise down the Green from Green River to the Confluence, then up the Colorado to Moab, provides an opportunity for everyone to get into the act. Water levels are high, and shallow water isn't much of a problem, but there have been groundings and damaged bottoms and motors.

For the purpose of this guidebook, I will leave the motors

Big Drop - Photo Eric Grohe courtesy Holiday River Expeditions

to others who use them—I don't—and deal with people-powered crafts.

CANOES: Canoes may be made of aluminum, wood, fiberglass, bark or synthetic material, each of which has its advantages as to price, durability, function, capacity, weight. I use an 18-foot Grumman canoe, which can carry me and my wife plus food, water and gear for several days on the river. A 17-footer would probably be a better river canoe for running rapids, but we paddle a lot of quiet water: lakes and Labyrinth Canyon and the Colorado both above and below Moab.

Several good books on canoeing include chapters on selecting a canoe. I like Bill Rivier's *Pole, Paddle & Portage*, which is currently being revised, but the newly-published American National Red Cross book *Canoeing* covers the subject briefly and well. Annual issues of *Canoe* magazine and occasional issues of *Down River* also deal with the matter of selecting a canoe that is best for you and your purpose.

KAYAKS: Kayaks have taken over many western rivers in the past decade. Before 1970 you rarely saw one, but today they are everywhere there is whitewater and a lot of places there isn't. Try Jay Evan's book *Kayaking* or the ANRC book *Canoeing* mentioned above; it also discusses kayaking. Both will provide the reader with background on and suggestions for selecting a kayak if that is the way you want to go. One of the best kayak builders lives in Utah just out of Canyon Country: Dick Held, Whitewater Boats, P.O. Box 483, Cedar City, UT 84720. He also builds canoes.

Kayaks are possibly the ultimate whitewater craft, but most kayakers get bored with flat water. Only a few stretches of rivers covered by this guidebook will be of interest to the kayaker: Westwater and Cataract Canyon on the Colorado, perhaps the San Juan and the Ruby Canyon stretch of the Colorado in Colorado and the upper Dolores in Colorado, possibly the Professor Valley stretch of the Colorado above Moab. Otherwise it's flat water all the way.

Kayaks normally carry only one person, the paddler, though there are K-2's (two-person kayaks). It's a great way to go, but it is strenuous and requires great skill. It is also expensive to take the whole family, especially here in Utah, if everyone has his own kayak. A canoe, by contrast, normally carries two and can often accomodate three, perhaps even four if gear is limited to lunch.

DORIES: A dory is a modified row boat with upswept bow and stearn, high, outward curving sides, and a small flat bottom. Its name comes from a Central American Indian word (dori or duri) meaning dugout, but the craft has come a long ways from its dugout days. Although relatively heavy and not at all portageable, it can be lined with ease and it floats like a cork. It is maneuverable and has a very shallow draft. It slices through the water much more rapidly than a raft on flat water.

Popular in the Pacific Northwest, especially in Oregon, where they are called McKenzie River boats or simply "drift boats," dories have been expanding their territory. One commercial outfitter uses them in the Grand Canyon and on other waters, and numerous northwesterners moving to other parts of the country — including Canyon Country — have taken dories and the dory idea along with them. They can run just about anything a raft can run and a lot more than an open canoe or even a sportyak can handle.

SPORTYAK: The sportyak, produced and sold by Dayton

Kayak on the river — Photo courtesy J. Dewell

Marine Products (7565 East McNichols Road, Detroit, MI 48234), is an indestructible unsinkable plastic bathtub-of-a-boat that can take some of the worst rapids in the West. Molded from bonded linear polyethylene, this tiny craft has been used in some of the wildest water of the Colorado River including Cataract Canyon and Grand Canyon. In fact, it is the smallest craft—7- or 8-feet long and 42 or 48-inches wide, depending on the model—even to have navigated the Colorado River through Grand Canyon (see the article on sportyaks, "A New Breed of Boat," by Cecil Kuhne in the September 1977 issue of *Down River* magazine). At least two commercial outfitters operating in Canyon Country run sportyaks trips; Fastwater Expeditions, Box 365, Boulder City, NV 89005, and Wild and Scenic, Inc., Box 2123, Marble Canyon, AZ 86036, and a third rents them for use on the Green River; Outlaw Trails, Inc., Box 336, Green River, UT 84525.

Sportyaks will obviously take rough water, but how are they in quiet water? Fine, but you have to work hard to make much mileage on flat water. The sportyak would be great for Westwater or Ruby Canyon or in Professor Valley, all on the Colorado, or for the San Juan. But you might have to work too hard to enjoy the Labyrinth-Stillwater run on the Green.

Since sportyaks are so small, a support boat of some kind is often used to carry most of the food and gear, water and clothing. It is a different way to go, paddling—or rowing—your own craft, flowing with the river, feeling it more than you would in any other kind of craft. The sportyak is light enough to portage and sturdy enough to take the bumps and bruises of some pretty big water. Try it; you'll like it.

EQUIPMENT: What will you need besides a craft?

First, some means of power and control: sweeps, oars, paddles, or a motor. Sweeps are oversized oars mounted on the ends of a craft and used to move the craft left or right as it drifts with the current, parallel to the flow. Oars are mounted at the sides of the craft; the rower sits facing downstream, pulling the oars to control the craft, perhaps to slow down its downstream movement to allow time to avoid a rock or souse hole. Dories and sportyaks are normally rowed with oars.

Large inflatables not powered by motors may be controlled by oars or sweeps, though sweeps have not been used much in Canyon Country. Smaller inflatables, the kind usually used in southeastern Utah and normally called "rafts", are almost always rowed with oars though many private parties use paddles.

Paddles are not mounted but are held in the hands of the paddler(s). Individual inflatables and small rafts, canoes and kayaks are usually paddled though you occasionally hear of someone who has mounted oars on a canoe or sweeps on a small raft. Kayaks are paddled with a double-bladed paddle and canoes, with a single bladed paddle. In addition, the kayak paddler sits, but the canoe paddler kneels. In fact, these two differences between kayaking and canoeing are the only basic differences between the two crafts today except for a few minor design features. The decked canoe is very similar to the kayak except for the kind of paddle and the position of the paddler. You can even do an Eskimo roll in a C-1 or C-2 (one-passenger or two-passenger decked canoe).

If you plan to use oars or sweeps, you will need a frame that you can make yourself or purchase from one of the river equipment outlets (try Walton Marine in Salt Lake City or Northwest River Supplies, Box 9243, Moscow, ID 83843) or have some professional carpenter or welder make for you (try Dean Waterman in Kanab, Utah). For oars and paddles, try the same outlets or those who advertise in *Canoe* and *Down River* magazines or those mentioned in the books listed in the bibliography.

Personal flotation devices are required by law. They must be Coast Guard approved and worn at all times on the river. Several types are available, different types required for different purposes. Research the field, find a safe comfortable PFD, and wear it. Don't use it for padding or for a pillow; don't sit or kneel on it. Such use may damage it beyond validity as a safety device. If the air-tight water-proof packet is broken, the life jacket may not support you. It could be a hazard rather than a help.

A bailing device of some kind should be carried: a plastic or metal bucket, a cut-down plastic bottle with a handle, or large sponge. To keep equipment and clothing dry, prevent sleepings from getting wet and to protect camera gear you'll need waterproof bags, boxes or containers of some kind. Military surplus stores and outlets that cater to river runners have a wide selection from which to choose. Check the ads in the river running magazines.

I use a Sport Safe by Recreation Creations, Inc. (Silver Lake Road, Dingmans Ferry, PA 18328) for my oversized

A triple rig - Photo courtesy Ray Varley

camera, Ann Dwyer's Klamath Rugged Pack (California Rivers, Box 468V, Geyserville, CA 95441) for clothing and sleeping bag, and Voyageur's (Box 512-V Shawnee Mission, KS 66201) waterproof canoe bags for almost anything small enough to fit into the 22" x 36" bag. Keep in mind that while hard-surfaced containers protect certain items better, they can create a hazard to passengers on a moving craft.

Military surplus ammunition cases are standard equipment for carrying many items from food to cameras on a river trip. I use a small one painted silver for a "possibles" container, especially for my film. Larger ones can be used for kitchen gear and food. Such ammo cans make good supports or bases for make-shift tables constructed on the camping beach from driftwood or plywood slabs carried along for that purpose.

Once again I suggest that you turn to other publications to magazines and books dealing with river running, rafting, canoeing, kayaking to dig out the equipment that is best for your own purpose. A detailed bibliography appears at the end of this guidebook. Use it to meet your needs for crafts and equipment. My own *River Running*, Bill McGinnis' *Whitewater*

A dory adapted for river running

Rafting, Rick Kremmer's *Guide to Paddle Adventure*, and several others are well worth reading not only for advice on boats and gear but to get the feel of the sport of river running.

If you want to get to know an area and what it has to offer, it pays to carry along a good river library with maps and books on geology, history, natural history, perhaps the stars, the prehistoric inhabitants of the area. And take along a notebook to record your own observations.

Wet suits are a must for cold-water or cold weather boating, especially if you kayak. I like wet boots for footgear while I am on the river. More and more river runners are using helmets when they run whitewater; for kayakers they are a must. Special accessories for specific kinds of river running you can get at specialty stores: items like spray skirts and helmets, wet suits and wet boots.

Generalized camping gear can be used for river trips though many people make their own kitchen boxes or food containers. Tents and sleeping bags should be lightweight and compact. Car-top carriers for canoes and kayaks and other gear can be purchased or constructed at home. Wet-weather

River camping - Photo courtesy F.A. Barnes

gear can be standard—nothing different on a river trip except that you get wet from below as well as above. Wear wool in cold weather; it insulates even when it is wet.

Safety devices such as throw lines or rescue bags can be found at most river runner specialty stores and are advertised in *Canoe* and *Down River* and *American Whitewater* and other publications. Magazines are better than books for keeping up with current equipment because it changes so often.

Backpackers in Coyote Gulch of the Escalante River

Logistics

Logistics is the business of moving, supplying, quartering, an appropriate word to describe what goes on behind the scenes of a river trip—the details that enable you to enjoy the actual time on the water, which, on a five-day trip, may be less than 30 hours. Logistics involves transportation including the shuttle, food and water supply, cooking and camping, disposal of trash and garbage and human waste, and simple river etiquette. The greatest time and effort of a river trip involves these logistical activities. Checklists should be used in every phase.

TRANSPORTATION: Getting to the launch site and home from the landing can be pretty routine though I recall taking out at Lathrop Canyon the summer of '77 after a canoe trip when the drive out was as slow as our progress on the river— 3½ miles an hour—for the first two hours. Some take-out points require four-wheel vehicles, but you can plan your trip for conventional vehicle access though to do so is to limit your choice of river trips.

Since you always end up somewhere other than where you start a river trip, you must plan a shuttle, an arrangement to get a vehicle from the starting point to the finish. This can be

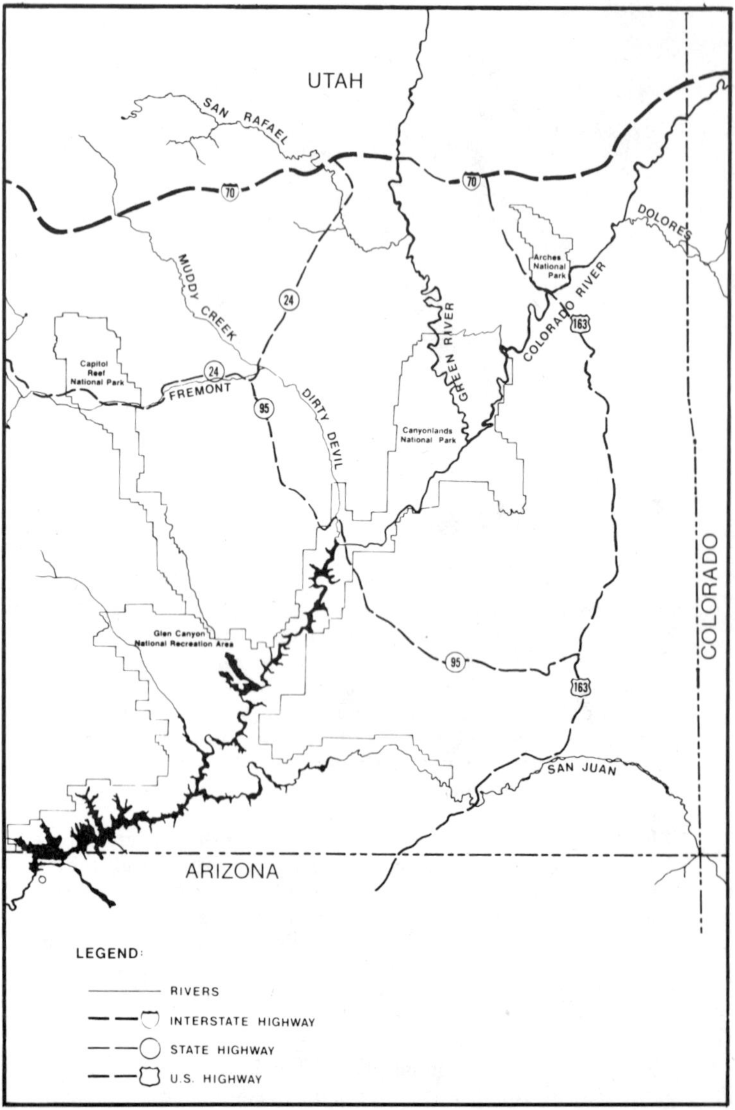
UTAH
SAN RAFAEL
70
70
DOLORES
MUDDY CREEK
24
Arches National Park
COLORADO RIVER
GREEN RIVER
163
Capitol Reef National Park
24
FREMONT
95
DIRTY DEVIL
Canyonlands National Park
COLORADO
Glen Canyon National Recreation Area
95
163
SAN JUAN
ARIZONA
LEGEND:
RIVERS
INTERSTATE HIGHWAY
STATE HIGHWAY
U.S. HIGHWAY

Carrying canoe on car top

done in any of several ways. You can take one car with an extra driver, a bit of a problem for trips of several days duration. You can hire a driver to drop you off at the river, then pick you up at the end of the trip, wherever that might be. You can hire a deadhead driver, someone to leave your vehicle at the end of the trip, but that requires two drivers, one to drive the deadhead driver back home.

Several commercial enterprises in Canyon Country — motel owners, touring services, river outfitting companies — provide shuttle service for a fee. Many professional river guides, when they are not on the river, may be available for shuttle service, and most of them know the shuttle roads to the river launch and take-out sites. I have paid $5 for a delivery to Ruby Ranch 23-miles down river from the town of Green River (30 miles one way) for a launch, $20 for a pick-up the next day at Mineral Bottom, a 140-mile roundtrip. Howard Valle of Valle's Trailer Park and Trading Post in Mexican Hat charges $25 for the shuttle to Clay Hills Crossing on the San Juan (about 70 miles), $50 for deadheading. Drivers are available in most of the river communities in the area.

Lunch on the Green in Labyrinth Canyon

FOOD AND WATER: What you eat on the river will depend to some extent upon what kind of craft you use and how long you plan to be on the river. Kayakers travel light. So do sportyakers unless they have a support boat along. Canoes can carry adequate food and equipment. Dories and rafts can carry the kitchen sink.

Go light to begin your river running experience, then add luxury as you desire and can handle. There is no need to eat backpacker fare on the river unless you want to. Some people prefer to do a minimum of cooking, using the time saved to explore side canyons, but others like to relax and enjoy a good meal even as they rough it.

Water is obviously available on the river, but it may not be palatable or safe. You can find springs and seeps and side-canyon streams on some of the Canyon Country rivers at some seasons, but even this you may want to treat. It is safest to carry your own water, a gallon per person per day, more in hot weather, perhaps a little less when it is cool. Canned and bottled beverages may add to your liquid supply and the weight of your load, but nothing can take the place of water.

COOKING AND CAMPING: Cooking on the river is little

Photo Duane Erickson courtesy Viking Explorer Canoes

different than outdoor cooking anywhere, but certain precautions should be followed and certain patterns practiced. Most professional river runners now use fire pans for their cooking and camping fires, a metal pan with raised edges to contain the ashes. Before breaking camp, the river runner can screen out all unburned or non-burnable material and haul it out with other non-burnable trash, dumping the ashes and charred sand into the river. This practise leaves no campfire scars on the beaches.

All garbage and trash should be burned or carried out. Liquid waste can be drained into a sandy sump, but it will attract insects and animals (skunks, for example, that may cause problems in camp). Solid human waste can readily be

Inflatable boats on trailer

carried out along with the non-burnable garbage and trash (see Steve Carothers' article "Let's Carry It All Out" in the August 1977 (Vol. 8, No. 6) issue of *Down River*).

Sandy beaches are the greatest places in the world to sleep. You just need to wiggle around a little to dig appropriate depressions in the soft sand that conform to your body, then drift off into a sound sleep with the sound of slowing waters lulling you to slumber. Tamerisk has so overgrown most of the Canyon Country riverbanks that it is difficult to camp on the benches above the river except in a relatively few places. High water camps are at a premium.

But for most of the year, the beaches are available. They show less wear and are normally replenished each spring. There is no need to scar the riverbank by removing vegetation to create a sleeping area. Natural openings are available, especially in frequently-used camping areas. The rivers can withstand a lot more human impact if we learn to take better care of their shorelines where we camp, carrying out everything we haul in and respecting the very nature of the area.

RIVER ETIQUETTE: River etiquette involves using common sense and practising responsibility on the river. Etiquette is

Loading up for a run down the Green River
Photo courtesy F. A. Barnes

defined as "the forms, manners, and ceremonies established by convention as acceptable." I won't stand on ceremony, but I will suggest that river etiquette requires certain responsibilities and conventions.

River users should leave their campsites at least as clean as they found them. We used to try to leave our camps so clean and undisturbed that we'd play games with other parties on the river to see if we could hide our camps from one another as we leap-frogged down the river.

I can't help mentioning Aldo Leopold's observation to the introduction to *Sand County Almanac:* "We abuse the land because we regard it as a commodity belonging to us. When we see land as a community to which we belong, we may begin to use it with love and respect." I would apply this concept to river camping. It we see the land as a community to which we belong, we can join the ancient ones who were a part of that community in our use of the land along the rivers.

It is inappropriate to throw litter into the river, to ruin the serenity of the scene with raucous noises — though I must admit to a penchant for calling forth echoes from the canyon walls. It is inappropriate to move in on another party already camped, perhaps at the site you had planned to use. It is inappropriate to engage another party in a water fight unless they want it as much as you do.

Basically river etiquette means being on your best behavior when you are on the river. The river resource belongs to all of us, and therefore to none of us; there are few people there to police us. But we shouldn't need policing if we use a little common sense and act responsibly, if we follow Aldo Leopold's suggestion, if we are on our best behavior — only because the river deserves that kind of respect.

NOTE: Many of the logistics specifics will be given in a following section on the specific rivers, information such as access points, shuttle arrangements, and times and distances. Other more general information on river running logistics can be gleaned from reading the books and magazines suggested in the bibliography. You can't learn to run a river by reading books, but you can gather much of the necessary background and knowledge, enough for you to learn to ask the right questions and even find the places to look for the answers.

Health and Safety

Health and safety considerations become vital on extended river trips in isolated canyons where any kind of help may be hours, even days away. Drinking water can cause problems as can lack of such basic practices as washing the hands and brushing the teeth. Safety factors on and off the river can mean the difference between a fun trip and a disaster.

The knowledge that help may be a long ways away in time and distance can help you plan the trip. Take any standard medication along, have a person along who knows basic first aid procedures, and be prepared for potential emergencies. Carry adequate drinking water and food, first aid supplies and anything else you might need including insect repellent, suntan lotion, dark glasses to protect the eyes against the glare of the sunlight off the water. Go prepared and practice common sense. Don't ever exert. Keep an eye on the weather. Don't get too much sun or too little safe water.

Off the river watch for snakes, spiders, scorpions, and other creepy crawly things that might sting or bite. Keep an eye out for cacti and thorn bushes of numerous variety that make up the desert vegetation. Tamerisk, the exotic Asiatic

Photo Kim Crumbo courtesy Holiday River Expeditions

plant that has grown wild along the riverbanks, can cause slivers when you break it for firewood, can stick you in the eye as you try to force your way through it. Be careful climbing the talus slopes at the foot of cliffs, or following steps cut by ancient Indians to cliff dwellings or doing any climbing on slickrock surfaces. Most accidents happen off the river. Be careful of slick rocks, loose rocks, sharp rocks, of the many natural hazards that exist in the river environment.

On the river wear your life jacket, especially if you decide to enter the river to cool off. Scout potentially dangerous rapids and run them cautiously. Line them or carry around if they are beyond your ability. It is best not to try to go too far in a day. Don't be afraid to stop early if you are tired, but don't run at night unless you know the river perfectly. Know basic river practices for avoiding dangerous situations—this you can learn by reading, but only when you have put theory into practice can you be sure you are doing the right thing.

Know what to do if you are caught in a reverse curler, a wave that breaks upstream and hold you or the craft in the current. Know how to avoid a flip—and how to right the craft if you should flip. Know that you lean toward the rock, rather than away from it, when your craft is pinned on it by the current. Know how to ferry and use an eddy to stop or maneuver.

How do you learn all these things? By reading about them in the books and magazines listed in the bibliography, then by going out on the river with someone who knows what he's doing, finally by doing it on your own in a gradual progression, learning from your mistakes and gaining experience.

River running is a serious business for all the fun you may have doing it. Many pleasant Sunday afternoons have been spoiled by a serious accident. See the American National Red Cross film "The Uncalculated Risk" available from the State Boating Director (Utah Division of Parks and Recretation, 1596 West North Temple, Salt Lake City, UT 84116) or from the Western River Guides Association (994 Denver Street, Salt Lake City, UT 84111).

What do you do if you find yourself in the water? Don't panic! It may be better to stay with the craft—or it may be best to head for shore as soon as possible, especially if the water is terribly cold as it may be in early spring. It will depend upon the specific situation. No sense in heading for shore if shore is a vertical cliff. If your craft is the only way out of a steep-walled narrow canyon miles from anywhere, you will want to consider staying with the boat, but don't let it pinch you against a rock as you both dash through a rapid. Don't let yourself be caught between a rock and a hard-hull.

And don't try to stand up in fast water. Swim or skull as close to shore as you can. Should you get a foot caught under a rock or in a crack, the current could drown you in two feet of water with a dozen people trying to help and no one able to reach you. Rivers can be dangerous, but they are less so if you get to know them and what they do. Watch them from shore. Watch what they do to debris floating on their surface. And again, read, read, read about rivers and the experiences of other river runners.

I don't mean to frighten anyone or seem over-cautious, but river running is no child's play. High water is fast water and often cold. Have you heard of hypothermia? It is loss of

BEWARE — on the river wear your life jacket

body heat, and it kills river runners every year—people who don't know about it and its subtle ways of sapping energy. It is less likely to kill in Canyon Country because of the relatively warm climate most of the year, but winter trips can experience it. So can early-spring trips when water temperatures are low from snow-melt run-off.

HYPOTHERMIA CHART

Water Temperature	Exhaustion/ Unconsciousness	Survival Time
Under 32.5	under 15 minutes	under 15/45 minutes
32.5-40	15-30 minutes	30-90 minutes
40-50	30-60 minutes	1-3 hours
50-60	1-2 hours	1-6 hours
60-70	2 to 7 hours	2-40 hours
70-80	3-12 hours	indefinite

One of the best books I have seen on water safety is the American National Red Cross 1977 publication, *Canoeing*. It covers not only canoeing but every aspect of the sport including rescue techniques, first aid, safety, and competitive paddling. It also has a chapter on kayaks and rafts, but since there is actually so little difference between canoes and kayaks today (except the position and the paddle), the book is valid for any paddling activity and for river running in general. Several books listed in the bibliography have excellent chapters on health and/or safety. ARTA's *River Guides' Manual*, which is not for sale but is available free to members of the American River Touring Association (1016 Jackson Street, Oakland, CA 94607), is an excellent handbook, not only on safety but on river running generally.

Photo Roy Taylor courtesy Holiday River Expeditions

Natural Information

For whatever reason people run rivers—for the thrills or the grandeur, the natural beauty or scenic solitude, the history or prehistory, the wildlife or wilderness—the natural world plays an important part. Understanding that natural world enhances the experience, expands the meaning of a river trip. Running rivers can be an end in itself or only a small part of learning about the region we have called Canyon Country in its entirety.

VEGETATION: Beginning with the vegetation—because that is where all life begins in Canyon Country—that turns sunlight and soil and water into food, we can see how vital the rivers are to the desert world. The Green River was so named by early Spanish explorers (Rio Verde) because, as John C. Fremont said, "The refreshing appearance of the broad river, with its timbered shores and green-wooded islands, in contrast to its dry sandy plains, probably obtained for it the name Green River, which was bestowed by the Spaniards, who first came into this country."

River vegetation has changed mightily since Fremont came through. Tamerisk, an import from the Mediterranean, has virtually taken over along all of the rivers of the region. A pest plant that develops into impenetrable jungles, the

Rabbit brush near the San Juan

tamerisk has long roots that seek the water level and can thrive better than many native plants. There is some suggestion that on reservoir-release rivers like the Green and San Juan and the Colorado below Glen Canyon Dam, native species are competing better as a result of the more stable flow and may even be coming back.

Those native species include various willows, reed grass, cattails and nettles, alders and cottonwoods. Not far from water may be found numerous other plant species including sagebrush near enough to supply beaver with food and building material, rabbitbrush not a dozen feet from the San Juan at Sand Island boat launch, cliffrose and squawbush, *Equisetum* (horsetail or scouringrush), and numerous species of cacti. Other common plants of the river marge include the whole pinyon-juniper habitat, blackbrush and greasewood, mountain mahogany and saltbush, snakeweed and Mormon tea (*Ephedra*), Gambel's oak and various berries. Off-river hiking can lead to many more desert species including the delicate rice grasses, colorful wildflowers blooming in seeps and springs — columbine, penstamen, orchids — as well as numerous hardy desert varieties of lupine, Indian paintbrush, composites.

Photo Duane Erickson courtesy Viking Explorer Canoes

Desert vegetation generally reacts more strongly to availability of water than to seasonal differences except for temperature. Of course, water available is largely a seasonal matter, but desert vegetation will respond to rain more quickly than to almost any other factor of weather or climate. Along the rivers where moisture is normally available the vegetation is more likely to exhibit characteristics of abundant water than most other desert plants.

ANIMALS: Many forms of wildlife are present along the rivers of the region, especially birdlife with dozens of species nesting in the willow and tamerisk thickets and numerous others nesting elsewhere in the high desert country. Signs of many species can be found along the river from beaver cuts and porcupine gnawings to coyote scat and badger dens. Tracks are abundant in the soft mud and silt at the edge of the river: racoon, beaver, deer, bighorn sheep, skunks, cats, a wide variety of birds from great blue heron to spotted sandpipers.

Mule deer come to the river for water and are frequently seen from the river as are bighorn sheep on the Green and Colorado rivers in Canyonlands National Park. Many desert species are more active at night than during daylight hours—

the badger and bobcat, the kit fox and coyote, the beaver and bat, various rodents and even a few birds like the great horned owl or the common nighthawk. Rabbits—both desert cottontails, which you are more likely to see during the day, and blacktailed jackrabbits, which are generally nocturnal— are common as is the porcupine where ever it finds food. One of the most conspicuous rodents is the whitetail antelope squirrel, a primary food supply for many of the high desert carnivores.

With the exception of the muskrat, which is normally less evident, the beaver more than any other animal lives along the river, leaving his signs: bank dens and lodges, tracks and drag marks, scent piles and fresh cuts on just about every kind of vegetation from cottonwoods to sagebrush. About dusk you can often see this huge water-going rodent swimming silently through the twilight or you can hear him when he slaps his tail on the water to warn fellow beavers of man's presence. You may see beaver feeding on willow twigs or waddling out of the river into a tamerisk thicket to cut breakfast.

A few amphibians—toads, frogs and salamanders—frequent the riparian habitat. I once saw—and later heard at a distance—a huge bullfrog with a bright yellow throat (as I was writing this, I asked my daughter, who was with me at the time, if she remembered it. Yes, she said, "It was big and green and had a yellow throat and it croaked loud."). Tree and chorus frogs often sing choruses at night, and both the Rocky Mountain toad (Woodhouse's) and the western spadefoot are common. Leopard frogs may also be found, often in backwater pools left by the falling water level after spring run-off. The Utah tiger salamander, a colorful critter, is also found along Canyon Country rivers.

Among the reptiles, numerous lizards live along the rivers, the most delightful and colorful being the collared, one of the few that runs on its hind legs like some of the ancient dinosaurs were supposed to have done. A strikingly colored green sub-species with a yellow head (*auriceps*) is found in Canyon Country. Other common lizards include the long-nosed leopard, the rare orange-headed spiny, the northern plateau, the northern sagebrush, the northern side-blotched, the tree, the mountain short-horned, the many-lined skink, the northern whiptail. Don't expect to see them all or identify any but the collared unless you are into herpetology and have a copy of Robert C. Stebbins' *Field Guide to Western*

Collared lizard

Reptiles and Amphibians along in your river library.

The Stebbins' book is also useful for snakes, of which there are not as many as the desert country might lead you to think. Though both are somewhat uncommon, the smooth green snake and the Painted Desert glossy snake may both be found along the San Juan and Colorado rivers. The striped whipsnake and the Great Basin gopher snake are both common along Canyon Country rivers, but the midget faded rattlesnake is the only rattler. Three other snakes you might find are the black-necked garter, the western terrestrial (wandering) garter, and the California kingsnake. The colorful milk snake, which the novice may take for a coral snake, may make an appearance as might the Mesa Verde nightsnake and the western black-headed snake.

BIRDS: Birdlife on the river produces excitement on every river trip I have ever been on, especially for those who know birds: white-throated swifts zooming along canyon walls, golden eagles soaring high overhead, canyon wrens offering their liquid double-descending song that seems like an oral waterfall, an ouzel bobbing on a rock in its frantic search for insects. The lovely violet-green swallow is often the most abundant bird on the river, especially just before a storm, and in spring the Audubon's warbler (now known as the yellow-rumped) appears in great numbers along the shore in the willow-tamerisk thicket.

Canada geese are common on the river as are half-a-dozen duck species: mallards, merganzers, green-winged teal, pintails, shovelers, golden-eyes, and a scattering of others flying through on spring migration. Hawks hunt the canyon benches for rodents, birds and insects: Cooper's, marsh, ferruginous, red-tailed, Swainson's, the prairie falcon and the kestrel. Owls take over at night: great-horned echoing their soft calls off the canyon walls, burrowing owls on the sandy flats, short-eared and long-eared owls nesting in the hollows.

For color we can count the belted kingfisher, rufous-sided towhee, Bullock's oriole, lazuli bunting, American avocet, barn swallow, cedar waxwing, scrub and pinyon jay, red-shafter flicker, yellow warbler, western tanager, blue grosbeak, and yellow-breasted chat. For song we have the black-headed grosbeak, mocking bird, warbling vireo, robin, mourning dove, western meadowlark, house finch, white-crowned sparrow and song sparrow. For size contrast we have the great blue heron and the ruby-crowned kinglet.

There are exotics too, imported species like the tamerisk: ring-necked pheasant, chukars and starling.

Along the river the spotted sandpiper flits from beach to beach, bobbing its tail when it lands. The black-and-white magpie sends its raucous screeching cry from thicket to thicket. The rock wren tries to compete with the canyon wren, both vocally and visually, and comes out second-best.

Brewer's blackbirds with an occasional red-wing adding a flash of color flock in the more civilized areas. The American bittern, black-crowned night heron, snowy egret and green heron, less common than the great blue heron, nonetheless occur, and the black tern appears at least in spring, the only season I have seen this lovely bird.

Along the river I have seen willet, kildeer and coot, common snipe, both eastern and western kingbirds, ravens, numerous cliff swallows that build their mud nests under overhanging cliffs along the canyon walls. Off the river I have seen Bewick's wren, western and ash-throated flycatchers, yellow-bellied sapsuckers, pine siskin, a number of different hummingbirds (Calliope, broad-tailed, black-chinned, rufous), hairy and downy woodpeckers, white-breasted nuthatches, common bushtit, tree swallows, Say's phoebe, horned larks, catbirds... the list goes on and on.

Birding is great along Canyon Country rivers, especially in the spring.

In addition to the mammals and birds, amphibians and reptiles, Canyon Country offers a wide variety of creepy crawly things, many of which bite or sting but are part of the wildlife scene. Mosquitoes are legion in the spring just after high water, and in the desert centipedes and scorpions abound. The black widow spider is common, and there is some evidence of the brown recluse's extending its territory in this direction (they have been found in nearby New Mexico and in Southern California). Tarantulas, while not poisonous to man, can — though rarely do — inflict a painful bite, but they are delightful creatures to observe and have become quite popular as pets in recent years.

The conenose kissing bug lives! I thought Ed Abbey was putting me on when I read Chapter 2, "The Great American Desert," in *The Journey Home*, but a little research on my part has borne him out. In May the winged adults of this species, which live and breed in the dens of woodrats, take flight and disperse, often coming in contact with man. Since they feed on animal blood, they may attack sleeping people on river trips and cause an itching sensation, even a burning pain, and in about 5% of the population, severe reaction that may even lead to anaphylactic shock and unconsciousness.

Ants, velvet ants (which are actually wingless wasps), wasps, hornets and bees (both honey and bumble), and yellowjackets all frequent the desert riparian habitat in Canyon Country. Don't fight them. Leave 'em alone and they'll go home, carrying their tails behind them. Deer flies and horse flies may be a bother at times, but they come with the territory. They are part of the price you pay to float western rivers.

A number of other non-stinging insects live in Canyon Country. Some even make tracks in the sand or mud. Others build unique or elaborate dwellings or leave their marks on rock or shrub or provide food for the insectivores. Dragonflies, mayflies, stoneflies, caddislies hatch in great numbers at certain seasons and may become a real nuisance at times. Water bugs and strides can be delightful to watch, but Mormon crickets, which normally roar forth in late spring can be dreadful. Butterflies and spiders add their color to the canyon scene too.

Fluted metamorphic rocks along the river

Fish in the normally-turbid waters of Canyon Country rivers include catfish, carp, suckers, shiners and a variety of exotic (transplanted) gamefish that have worked their way up the rivers from Lake Powell, where they have been planted. The Colorado squawfish, bonytail and humpback chub and humpback sucker are all considered rare or endangered species.

GEOLOGY: I am not a geologist though I once taught earth science to high school students. However, I do not feel qualified to compete with the experts who have already written river runners' guide to the geology of the Colorado, Green and San Juan rivers. Whatever I might have to say here would be superfluous. Allow me to generalize to this extent: the Canyon Country rivers flow through the Colorado Plateau, having cut deep canyons through massive layers of relatively flat Jurassic, Triassic, Permian and Pennsylvanian sediments. Some were deposited by wind; others, by water. They are colorful, varying from deep reds through pinks, oranges and yellows to pale pastel greens and grays. They are impressive.

The best layman books on the geology of the area have been done by geologists who are also river runners. They may be slightly too technical for a few, but anyone interested enough in floating the Canyon Country rivers owes it to him/herself to learn a little about the geology of the area. Try Felix E. Mutschler's *River Runners' Guide To Canyonlands National Park and Vicinity*, which covers the Green River from Green River, Utah (I-70) to the Confluence and the Colorado from Moab, Utah to a point below Hite Marina on Lake Powell. Published by the Powell Society Ltd. of Denver, this book has an excellent glossary.

For the San Juan there is *Geology of the Canyons of the San Juan River* by D. L. Baars, a river runner's guide published by the Four Corners Geological Society. Baars has also produced *Geology of Canyonlands and Cataract Canyon*. Brigham Young University has produced a *Guidebook to the Colorado River*, Part 3, which covers the Colorado River from Moab to the mouth of the Dirty Devil River on Lake Powell, a distance of 111 miles.

HISTORY: When the Dominquez-Escalante Expedition made their loop through the Colorado Plateau in 1776, they crossed all of the major Canyon Country rivers — the San Juan, the Dolores, the Green, and the Colorado — but they did so, for the most part, outside the area considered by this guidebook. Only the Colorado did they cross in this immediate area, but the famed "Crossing of the Fathers" has been drowned by Lake Powell and is difficult to trace today.

Perhaps the first evidence of Western Civilization on the rivers of Canyon Country was left by the French trapper Denis Julien, who ascended the Colorado and Green Rivers the spring of 1836, leaving his name and the dates of his visit at several places along the way, carved into the rock walls of the canyons.

In 1853 Lt. John Gunnison led a party across the Green River near present-day Green River. He was killed by Indians only a few days later, but his name has lived in Gunnison Butte just north of Green River, which was known as Gunnison Crossing for many years. In 1855 Mormon settlers tried to establish a community at Moab but were driven away by local Indians.

Major John Wesley Powell led his exploration of the Green and Colorado rivers through the area the spring and summer of 1869 and again in 1871-72. He was absent from much of this second trip, but his men conducted major explorations in the area. A. H. Thompson, Powell's brother-in-law, discovered the Escalante River in 1872 and named the Henry Mountains for Joseph Henry, Powell's benefactor at the Smithsonian Institution. Jacob Hamblin, Brigham Young's apostle to the Indians, had done a lot of exploring in Canyon Country but had not found a way to the mouth of the Dirty Devil River, where Powell had hoped to be re-supplied on his second expedition, nor had he found the Escalante River, which Powell had missed on his 1869 expedition though he floated right past it. Thus, the Escalante was the last river in the West to be discovered.

The San Juan River was run as early as 1882 by an oil prospector, E. L. Goodridge; by Bert Loper, an early river runner, in 1893 or 94; by Walter E. Mendenhall, a gold prospector for whom the Mendenhall Cabin at the Goosenecks is named, in 1894. A successful oil well was drilled in the San Juan Basin in 1908, a year before nearby Rainbow Bridge was discovered, and the first scientific exploration of the area occurred in 1921 when the Trimble Expedition studied the area from the river.

The Green River was bridged by the Denver and Rio Grande Western Railroad in 1883, and a small town grew up there numbering fifty people in 1889, when Robert Bruster Brown and Frank M. Brown a river trip at Green River, Utah to explore the canyons downstream for a possible railroad route. Brown was drowned in Marble Canyon just below Soap Creek Rapid, and the route was abandoned.

Prospectors, trappers, geologists, map-makers began to use the river as a route to reach unexplored places. Steamboats were used to haul equipment in or ore out for various mining operations looking for everything from gold to uranium. The surrounding area became cattle country, outlaw country. Various early river runners made occasional trips on various Canyon Country streams.

In 1926 Ellsworth Kolb, a Grand Canyon boater, joined Bert Loper to run Westwater Canyon. Harold H. Leich kayaked the Colorado from Grand Lake to Grand Junction in 1933, then soloed Westwater in a wooden punt Aug. 16 the same year—according to Dock Marston, river historian. Marston, Don Harris, Bert Loper, Norman Nevills, Georgie WhiteKen Ross, Frank Swain and Bus Hatch—these were the old time river runners using wooden cataract boats. Nat Galloway of the upper Green and Yam-a taught them to run the rivers stern first, but they taught themselves to run the rapids of the San Juan and the Colorado, the mighty rapids of Cataract Canyon, which are bigger and better than those in Grand Canyon, at least at high water, which the Grand Canyon is not likely to see again because of Glen Canyon Dam.

By the mid-1930's most of the Canyon Country rivers had been run, not regularly or frequently but they had all become known quantities. In the mid-1940's with surplus military boats and pontoons suddenly available, rubber boats came into being as river crafts, and by the mid-1950's the boom had begun. Some people feel that Glen Canyon Dam actually started the boom in river running, that it made the Colorado below the dam safe for float trips, and as Grand Canyon became crowded, the pioneers, at least some of them, moved elsewhere—to Cataract Canyon, then to Westwater, to the Green and the San Juan and other parts of the Colorado. There is hardly a mile of major river in Canyon Country today that does not have a commercial float trip running it sometime during the year. Many stretches are so popular that they are badly overused.

However, many commercial operators overlook quiet waters because they are slow and dull compared to the rapids. These areas are ideal for canoeing. The San Juan has less traffic than other rivers because its flow is lower, controlled by a dam far upriver. It is an ideal river for sportyaks, for experienced canoeists. There are many miles of runable rivers in Canyon Country, and every run follows a historic route of some sort.

More than that, every route follows the route of the ancient ones, the prehistoric Indians who lived here centuries ago but left interesting evidence of their lives along Canyon Country rivers.

Canoers a few miles above Moab

Colorado River

Until 1921 the Colorado River above its confluence with the Green River was known as the Grand River (thus Grand Lake near its headwaters, Grand Junction, and Grand Valley). It flows roughly 145 miles through southeastern Utah before it dies in the impounded waters of Lake Powell. Except for a twelve-mile segment near Cisco, Utah, a ten-mile stretch through Professor Valley north of Moab, and the fifteen-mile stretch known as Cataract Canyon just above Lake Powell, it is flat water most of the way, ideal for canoeing but pleasant for almost any kind of boating from inflatables to dories, from kayaks to power boats. There is even a modern steamboat running the river near Moab.

The Colorado River to the mouth of the Dolores River, a major tributary stream, is currently under study for possible inclusion in the National Wild and Scenic Rivers System. It forms the southeastern boundary of Arches National Park and flows through Canyonlands National Park and Glen Canyon National Recreation Area. Its major tributaries in Utah besides the Dolores mentioned above, which is also under consideration for Wild and Scenic Rivers designation, are the Green, which joins the Colorado within Canyonlands National Park and is covered in this guidebook, and the San Juan, which flows into Lake Powell in Glen Canyon National Recreation Area (it once flowed into the Colorado River in Glen Canyon).

SEGMENTS: Several segments: Horsethief/Ruby Canyon that begins in Colorado but ends in Utah; Westwater Canyon; Westwater-to-Moab including the Professor Valley segment; Moab to the Confluence; and Cataract Canyon, the best whitewater in the State of Utah.

TYPE OF CRAFTS: small rafts for all of it, kayaks for the whitewater stretches, canoes for everything but Cataract Canyon, dories and sportyaks for everything.

MILEAGE: 26 miles for the Loma, Colorado to Westwater Ranch segment (Horsethief/Ruby Canyon); 17 miles for Westwater Canyon; 46 miles from the end of Westwater to Moab; 64 miles from Moab to the Confluence; 15/16 from the Confluence to Lake Powell, depending on water level in the reservoir.

TIME: 1 day, possibly 2 for Horsethief/Ruby Canyon; 1 day or 2 for Westwater (can be done in one, but it makes a nice weekend trip); 2 days from the end of Westwater to Moab; total time from Loma, Colorado to Moab (89 miles) 4 or 5 days. Moab to the Confluence 3 or 4 days; Moab to Lake Powell, 4 or 5 days or more depending on off-river activities.

USGS MAPS: in Colorado: Mack, Ruby Canyon (7½'); on Colorado-Utah stateline: Bitter Creek Well, Westwater 4 SE (7½'); in Utah: Westwater 4 SW, Danish Flat (7½') and Coates Creek, Cisco, Castle Valley, Moab, Hatch Point, Upheaval Dome, The Needles, Orange Cliffs, Mouth of Dark Canyon, Brown's Rim (15').

OTHER MAPS: Belknaps' *Canyonlands River Guide*, which covers the entire reach of the Colorado River in Canyon Country including Lake Powell; for geologic information and maps, Mutschler's *River Runners' Guide to Canyonlands National Park and Vicinity* covers the Colorado from Moab to Lake Powell.

HAZARDS: Rapids in Ruby Canyon, Westwater Canyon, Professor Valley and Cataract Canyon (*Note:* Rapids in Cataract Canyon are the biggest in the state, especially during high water periods, usually May and June); lack of potable water.

SEASON: The Colorado, at least in selected bits and pieces, can be run throughout the year, but the basic season is late March through October. It is best in May and June. Extended trips during the winter months can be uncomfortable, even dangerous, and I know of one party that had to walk out at the Doll House because Lake Powell was frozen over. Plan carefully.

ACCESS: The Loma, Colorado, I-70 Exit (south of highway by way of a gravel road along the river); Westwater Ranch, BLM access area off I-70 just south-west of Colorado-Utah stateline (Harley Dome); Rose Ranch (Hallet Ranch) south of Cisco on dirt road known locally as Pumphouse Road for the old Denver and Rio Grand pumphouse (shown on Multipurpose Map 2, Southeastern Central Utah); several places along U-128 between Dewey Bridge and Moab; west side of river (right bank) above U.S. 163 bridge near Moab; end of scenic road (U-279) downstream from Moab below Potash; four-wheel-drive access at Lathrop Canyon in Canyonlands National Park; Hite Marina on Lake Powell.

SHUTTLE: A two-car trip can be shuttled by the participants, but because of the long distances involved and the hassle, it may be wise to hire a driver. Shuttle arrangements can be made through local residents and ranchers or professional river runners in the area, especially in Green River and Moab. As an example, when I canoed from Loma, Colorado, to Westwater Ranch, I hired a boatman from an outfitter headquartered in Green River to drive with me to the put-in near Loma. He simply drove my car around to Westwater Ranch, where his own trip was putting in that same day, and left the car for my use when the trip ended. Don't forget to arrange a place to leave the car keys or use a second set.

The shuttle is complex and time-consuming. I prefer to hire the shuttle than to lose river time, but if you can arrange for a second driver who does not go along on the river trip, fine.

SUMMARY: The Loma, Colorado to Westwater segment, a good canoeing stretch, lies largely in Colorado. It begins in open ranchlands but soon enters a pastel sedimentary gorge known as Horsethief Canyon, which gives way without noticeable break to Ruby Canyon. Pinyon-juniper vegetation dominates the scene above the river, but the riparian habitat is varied offering excellent bird habitat. Ruby Canyon consists of pale sedimentary layers above dark metamorphic rocks that have been carved and fluted by the river into grotesque and exotic shapes reminiscent of the Vishnu schist of the inner gorge of the Grand Canyon, to which it is related.

There are several good campsites along the river. The Denver and Rio Grande Railroad traverses a portion of this run, and trains make scheduled run through the canyon. D&RG seems to have used the isolated canyon for a dumping grounds for the railroad fill is badly littered with all kinds of trash. Several four-wheel-vehicle roads reach the lower end of the run from either side of the river.

Westwater Canyon is one of the most popular runs in the state. Use has increased tremendously since the early 1970's when hardly anyone was running the stretch also known as Hades or Granite Canyon. It has some of the best rapids (Class III through V) in the state and is normally run by rafts and kayaks though sportyaks and dories would also be acceptable crafts here. Only the most experienced expert should try it in an open canoe, and the option to portage or line should be seriously considered, especially for Skull Rapid.

The first three miles below the BLM launch area flows slowly through open irrigated farmland. Then the river picks up speed and enters a canyon of dark Precambrian schist topped with redrock formations of Entrada Sandstone, Carmel Formation, Navajo Sandstone and Kayenta Formation. Only a few mild rapids and riffles change the pattern of flow above the mouth of the Little Dolores, the best campsite in the canyon, but at that point begins a series of a dozen rapids (Class II through V) in five miles including Funnel Falls, Skull or Cisco Bend, and Sock-It-To-Me. Then the water quiets and slows, emerging from the canyon four miles downstream. The take-out is two miles below the mouth of the canyon (see Utah Multipurpose Map 2 (H-3) for the road to Hallet Ranch (Rose Ranch on the Belknap River Guide).

From the river access at the old Denver and Rio Grande pump-station, it is roughly 46 miles to Moab with plenty of access points along the way after you reach the mouth of the Dolores River. From Dewey Bridge on U-128 the road parallels the river all the way to Moab, most of the time within a few feet. In the 12-mile stretch through Professor Valley, one of the most scenic areas, there are several access points by four-wheel-drive vehicle and at least two campsites frequently used by river runners.

A series of five rapids in the Professor Valley segment — Onion Creek, Professor Creek, New Rapid (at the fold of the Belknap River Guide), Ida Gulch and Castle Creek (or White's) Rapid — offer a challenge to the paddler, but I have run the

Cataract Canyon coming up - Photo courtesy Ray Varley

entire stretch in an open canoe with a novice in the bow without serious mishap—though we did dent the keel on a rock in Ida Gulch, and we ran the left side of the island in the second part of Ida Gulch (the right side runs into a cliff, creating a dangerous situation).

Below the mouth of Castle Creek the river enters a canyon again. There are a few riffles, perhaps the most serious at the mouth of Salt Wash, but here again I have run this stretch in an open canoe with a novice in the bow and had no trouble. From Salt Wash to Moab this stretch borders Arches National Park. The best take-out is on the right bank just above the bridge (U.S. 163) across the Colorado.

From Moab to the Confluence the Colorado is quiet. You

Whitewater! Cataract Canyon
Photo Kim Crumbo courtesy Holiday River Expeditions

can put in at the take-out point mentioned in the previous paragraph or at the end of the road (U-279) below Potash. Ideal for canoeing if you can arrange a four-wheel-drive vehicle pick-up at the mouth of Lathrop Canyon or a jetboat pick-up at the Confluence, this segment is slow and placid. There are Indian ruins, dinosaur tracks, ancient petroglyphs, a few arches, and good birding. Golden eagles nest along this segment, and great blue herons fish in the shallow muddy water. The only rapid is a mile-and-a-half above the Confluence where the Slide constricts the river from the right to form a narrow riffle on the left that can be lined if necessary.

Mutschler's *River Runners' Guide to Canyonlands National Park* augments the Belknaps' River guide from Moab on down, providing excellent geological background, a few historical notes and information of general interest. The canyon is not continuous. The river winds and loops through relatively open country that provides good views of Pyramid Butte, Dead Horse Point, and several other prominent features. Side canyon hiking can be rewarding with several small ruins perched on low cliffs not far from the river. If you go beyond Lathrop Canyon, the last access point above Cataract Canyon, you must either paddle or motor up the

Big Drop Rapid in Cataract Canyon—
Photo Kim Crumbo courtesy Holiday River Expeditions

Green or the Colorado, get a jetboat pick-up at the Confluence, or run the rapids of Cataract Canyon. Don't unless you are totally prepared to do so.

Campsites are abundant. Beaver are plentiful. The lower thirty miles lie in Canyonlands National Park.

So does Cataract Canyon, the best whitewater stretch in Utah. More than twenty named rapids including the extensive Mile Long Rapid (six rapids in less than a mile) and the Big Drop at the point where Canyonlands National Park gives way to Glen Canyon National Recreation Area. The lower part of the Big Drop is inundated by Lake Powell at maximum water level (3700 foot elevation), a point that is more than 200 river miles from Lees Ferry and 185 miles from Glen Canyon Dam.

The first 3½ miles below the Confluence is calm, but where the river makes a dog-leg to the left at the lower end of Spanish Bottom, a favorite camping spot on the right, the cataracts begin in rapid succession: ten rapids in four miles, 25 in eleven miles. Several inscriptions record part of the river running history of this canyon, the earliest going back to 1891 (a Denis Julien inscription from 1836 has been drowned by Lake Powell). Powell, during his 1869 expedition, made only ¾ mile one day when forced to make three successive portages in a stretch that he calculated dropped 75 feet. Actually the Colorado drops sixty feet in less than a mile-and-a-half in the Big Drop.

NOTES: Anyone who runs the Colorado should know something about the man who led the first — and second — exploration of its whitewater canyons: John Wesley Powell, who named many of the features that we see today. The spring of 1869 this one-armed veteran of the Battle of Shilo, where he lost an arm, launched three wooden boats into the Green River at Green River, Wyoming, and floated all the way down the Green to its confluence with the Grand (now the Colorado). From this confluence the Colorado had its beginning in Powell's day, and he followed it right on down Cataract Canyon, through Glen Canyon and the series of canyons we know collectively today as the Grand Canyon.

Of Glen Canyon, which he named, he said "A gorge beyond description. The walls are nearly vertical, the river broad and swift, but free from rocks and falls. From the edge of the water to the brink of the cliffs it is 1600 to 1800 feet." And yet there are rocks and falls in the canyon above Glen Canyon. Of Cataract Canyon he said "Large rocks have fallen from the walls — great angular blocks, which have rolled down the talus and are strewn along the channel.... Among these rocks, in chutes, whirlpools, and great waves, with rushing breakers and foam, the water finds its way."

The bighorn sheep that Powell saw more than a hundred years ago are represented by their progeny that still live along these canyon walls. And those who follow in Powell's path upon the river are represented by the hundreds and thousands who float the Colorado every year.

LAKE POWELL: The lower end of Cataract Canyon and all there was of Glen Canyon have been inundated by the rising waters of Lake Powell, named for the man who first floated the Colorado's free-flowing waters through these canyons. As the reservoir is drawn down for power production, it leaves a silty quicksand, massive mud flats that defy navigation or negotiation: you cannot walk or swim, paddle or row at times. According to Ken Ross, who knew the Colorado before the dam and who still floats the San Juan as far as Lake Powell will let him, the silt beds "wick up the water" to produce tremendous evaporation losses and high humidity on the upper reaches of the reservoir. Most river runners come prepared with a small outboard motor to power out across the lake to a take-out at Hite Marina more than 30 miles down the reservoir. Concessionaires at Hite can provide the service for a fee.

Some of the canyons on the upper reservoir are well worth exploring: Gypsum Canyon on the left; Clearwater Canyon on the right with its large waterfall and plunge pool a mile-and-a-half up the canyon; Bowdie Canyon on the left with its series of falls and plunge pools, a deep winding canyon; Dark Canyon, a lovely winding canyon that always has water (a hike up this spectacular canyon leads to the BLM's Dark Canyon Primitive Area). Each of these side canyons offers a unique experience. Any of them can take you away from the noise of the power boats if you hike a ways into their secret recesses. All of them are worth exploring if you have the time — and it's worth taking the time.

NOTES: The rapids in Ruby and Westwater Canyons and through Professor Valley should be scouted on a first run and at unknown water levels. I lined a rapid in Ruby Canyon on my first run. All can be portaged or lined with the possible exception of Skull and Sock-It-To-Me in Westwater, but this stretch is not recommended for open canoes or inexperienced paddlers.

There are numerous campsites along the river between Loma and Moab, most of them on public land, but be a careful thoughtful camper wherever you stop for the night. Carry out whatever you take in, and leave the river in good shape.

Canoeing in Labyrinth Canyon

Green River

The Green River flows 370 miles through eastern Utah, 120 miles of it south of I-70 and consequently within the scope of this guidebook. Named by the early Spaniards Rio Verde but known to the mountainmen as the Skeedskadee (prairie chicken), the Green has played an important part in the discovery, growth and development of the state. It was explored before the Colorado, even by Powell, and it has been the cradle of river running in the West along with the Colorado.

Its entire course through Canyon Country is calm quiet water that can easily be canoed by even the beginner if he has proper instruction and leadership, and its waters are amenable to almost any kind of craft used in or on any other waters of the state from the power boats that run in on the annual Friendship Cruise on Memorial Day Weekend to the various individual paddle craft like the sportyak, kayak or inflatable canoe.

SEGMENTS: from the town of Green River, Utah to the confluence with the Colorado River in Canyonlands National Park (including Labyrinth and Stillwater canyons).

TYPE OF CRAFTS: all: kayak, canoe, sportyak, raft (big and small), dory.

MILEAGE: 120 miles according to Belknaps' *Canyonlands River Guide,* 117.5 according to Mutschler's *River Runners' Guide* with emphasis on geologic features. I use them both but find the former indispensible.

TIME: 4 or 5 days, the current normally varies between 3 and 5 mph for an average of 30 hours of actual river time if you merely drift with the current, but side canyon hiking and other exploration may add to that time requirement appreciably. I have run the 45-mile segment from Ruby Ranch (opposite the mouth of the San Rafael) to Mineral Bottom on a 2-day weekend but prefer to have 3 days to allow more time to enjoy this beautiful stretch of quiet river in colorful canyons.

USGS MAPS: Green River, Bow Knot Bend, The Spur (15').

OTHER MAPS: Belknaps' *Canyonlands River Guide* covers the whole stretch of the Green in Canyon Country in detail. Southeastern Central Utah Multipurpose May 2 covers the entire region and shows access roads and the general geography of the area. Mutschler's *River Runners' Guide to Canyonlands National Park and Vicinity* has maps that help the river runner follow the geologic story of the area. I carry them all when I am on the river.

HAZARDS: primitive and remote, no potable water much of the year, Cataract Canyon lies downstream from the confluence with the Colorado (plan a take-out before you reach the confluence or a pick-up by jetboat at the confluence if you don't plan to run Cataract Canyon).

SEASON: The Green can be run any month of the year, but it may be cold from November through February or March. It is best in May and June through April can be nice most years. It gets terribly hot in summer, and while the water is normally low in the fall, the autumn colors along the river make it an ideal time to run—and there aren't many people after Labor Day.

ACCESS: The major put-in is the boat ramp at Green River State Park in Green River, Utah, but some parties put in at Ruby Ranch, a private working ranch that charges $5 per boat and $1 per person to launch. It can be reached by driving 14 miles east of Green River and following a dirt road southwest about 15 miles to the river (see Multipurpose map). At four-wheel-drive road down Spring Canyon 13 miles from U-313 at Sevenmile Canyon 13 miles northeast of Moab reaches the river. A normal put-in point for Cataract Canyon trips and a take-out for trips that want to avoid Cataract Canyon is at

Petroglyph of bighorn sheep at mile 83 on the Green River

Mineral Bottom, accessible by conventional vehicle by dirt road from U-313 from a turn-off at Big Flat on the paved road to Dead Horse Point.

SHUTTLE: If you use two cars, you can shuttle yourself, but because of the dead-end roads involved you will use a lot of time. It may be worth more to you to hire someone to deliver you and your gear to the river at a put-in point, then meet you at the end of the trip, wherever that may be (Hite Marina on Lake Powell if you plan to run Cataract Canyon). Keep in mind the alternatives you have *if you do not plan to run Cataract Canyon:* take out at Mineral Bottom (it is the last chance), hire a jetboat pick-up at the Confluence, or plan to paddle or motor up either the Green or the Colorado to a logical take-out point upstream.

SUMMARY: Launching at Green River State Park, you will soon pass beneath the Denver and Rio Grande Western Railroad Bridge at the south end of town. The river drops only 180 feet between Green River and the Confluence, an average of only 1½ feet per mile, a slow river with flat water all the way. A few miles below Green River Crystal Geyser appears on the left bank, the result of a 1936 dry hole gar and oil well. The river flows through open ranchlands for most of the first 28 miles, occasionally bordered by low cliffs on one side or the other, rarely through anything like a real canyon. The San Rafael River comes in from the right 23 miles below Green River immediately across the Green from the launch site at Ruby Ranch (private). Five miles below that point, the river enters Labyrinth Canyon.

Labyrinth Canyon is one of the finest river canyons I have floated in my twenty years of running rivers. It is calm and peaceful, a scenic wonder without parallel. For 62 miles the Green flows through a series of loops in a colorful canyon with walls actually overhanging in places and rising several hundred feet into the desert sky where sheep-like clouds drift lazily along, their bottoms pink from the reflected light off the redrock land below.

Two miles into the canyon at the outside of the first tight bend lies a fantastic side canyon that Powell called Trin-Alcove Bend. It is worth exploring at any season. During spring high water levels you can actually paddle a hundred yards or more into the canyon, which splits into three canyons, each more exciting than the last. Powell and his men camped on the sandy beach opposite this side stream, which fascinated them. They climbed to the rim to observe the surrounding countryside as you can too and as Mutschler suggests you do to see "all the geological formation crossed since leaving Green River."

Mutschler also suggests that "Since the filling of Lake Powell in Glen Canyon, this stretch on the Green is the last remaining canyon in Navajo Sandstone with undisturbed side canyons." (page 23)

Petroglyphs, both ancient and modern, and several inscriptions can be found along the canyon walls in many places. A river register used by boaters for decades is visible from the river on the left bank between miles 77 and 78 (Belknaps' river guide, 75.9 in Mutschler's). Two of the Denis Julien inscriptions can be found in Labyrinth Canyon, one visible from the river on the left bank between miles 74 and 75 (Belknap) or at 72.7 (Mutschler) (8 or 10 feet above the river but below the mining road along the river) and one a short distance up Hell Roaring Canyon. Julien, a Frenchman, left his name at several points along the Colorado and Green rivers on an upstream journey the spring of 1836. At one point—Bow Knot Bend—the river flows 7 miles to double back on itself less

Preparing to launch at Ruby Ranch

Bowknot Bend - Photo courtesy Bill Belknap

than half a mile from its upstream course.

A good take-out point at Mineral Bottom on the left offers the last access by road above Lake Powell and Cataract Canyon. Many of the commercial rafting companies launch their Cataract Canyon trips here. Just below mile 47 (Belknap) at Saddle Horse Bottom the river enters Canyons National Park. A few miles downstream at Fort Bottom an old "outlaw cabin" provides a good excuse for river runners to stop. On the bench above it a masonry tower dominates the scene and offers a fine view of the surrounding countryside, both upstream and down.

Labyrinth Canyon ends at mile 31 (Belknap) where an ancient entrenched meander was cut off by the river leaving another of many rincons or abandoned ox-bows. From here to the Confluence Stillwater Canyon takes over. Cliff dwellings appear here and there along the canyon walls, and several interesting rock formations—The Sphinx, Turks Head, the Butte of the Cross—offer food for the imagination. Of stillwater Canyon Powell wrote the third week of July, 1869, "Late in the afternoon the water becomes swift and out boats make great speed. An hour of this rapid running [not running rapids] brings us to the junction of the Grand [Colorado] and

The Confluence - Photo courtesy Bill Belknap

the Green, the foot of Stillwater Canyon, as we have named it."
NOTES: If you are not prepared to run the rapids of Cataract Canyon, do not go below the Confluence. The rapids begin four miles downstream just below a hard left turn, and the trail to the Doll House in the rim from Spanish Bottom begins 3½ miles below the Confluence, a logical place for a jetboat pickup. Don't attempt to run the rapids unless you have the proper craft and equipment and vast heavy whitewater experience.

River water is usually muddy and often unpalatable as well as unsafe for drinking. It can be chemically treated, but it may be better to haul enough water along for the whole trip at the rate of a gallon per person per day.

POWELL'S COMMENTS: A few of Major Powell's choice words may be in order here: "The line," he says, "that separates Labyrinth Canyon from the one below (Stillwater) is but a line," suggesting that his differentiation is an arbitrary one. "In many places the walls, which rise from the water's edge, are overhanging on either side. The stream is still quiet, and we glide along through a strange, weird, grand region. The landscape everywhere, away from the river, is of rock—ten thousand strangely carved forms; rocks everywhere, and no vegetation, no soil, no sand. In long gentle curves the river winds about these rocks...all highly colored—buff, gray, red, brown, and chocolate, never lichened, never moss-covered, but bare and often polished."

A FINAL NOTE ON LOGISTICS: Logistics, especially the shuttle, can be a real problem because of the long off-road-vehicles distances involved or the possibility of a take-out on Lake Powell. There are professional services available both among the commercial outfitters in Green River and Moab and the concessionaires in Glen Canyon National Recreation Area (note that it is illegal for a river outfitter to provide services to any but his own clients on Lake Powell). The services include vehicle shuttling, pick-ups both on the river and at take-out points, re-supplying, and many other useful activities, but they will cost you. However, the services are normally well worth the prices asked.

San Juan River

Little known outside of the Four Corners states, the San Juan is a mighty river in its own right, a major tributary of the Colorado that has carved a canyon equally as impressive as those carved by the Green and the Colorado. It rises in the San Juan Mountains of southern Colorado, is fed by numerous streams along the Colorado-New Mexico stateline (the Navajo, the Piedra, the Animas, the La Plata, the Mancos), flows within a mile of Four Corners Monument and for nearly 150 miles across southeastern Utah into Lake Powell.

It is dammed above Farmington, New Mexico to form Navajo Reservoir and supplies irrigation water for thousands of acres of Indian lands in the Four Corners Area. Its flow through Utah is regulated to a large extent by reservoir releases because tributary streams supply little additional water except during the spring snow-melt run-off. A minimum flow of 530 cubic feet per second (cfs) is not uncommon. Low water and the drowning of much of the San Juan's lower canyon by Lake Powell have reduced the number of commercial companies offering float trip service on the San Juan, but its turbid waters are almost ideal for intermediate canoeing use and sportyaks, and kayakers from all over the country come to the San Juan in high water for the sand waves.

A major corridor of ancient human movement between Mesa Verde and points south and west, the San Juan is probably the best remaining—now that Glen Canyon is no more—archaeological run in the state, especially below Bluff though its entire course through Utah offers extensive sign of ancient peoples.

SEGMENTS: Three segments will be discussed covering the entire San Juan River in Utah: 1) Four Corners to Sand Island (near Bluff), 2) Sand Island to Mexican Hat, and 3) Mexican Hat to Lake Powell.

TYPE OF CRAFTS: small rafts, sportyaks, open canoes, dories, kayaks.

MILEAGE: Section 1 = 55 miles (estimated), Section 2 = 28 miles (according to Baars), Section 3 = 56 miles (according to Baars).

TIME: Section 1 will take two long or three moderate days, Section 2 will take a long day except by kayak, Section 3 will take three or four days, longer if you plan to do much side canyon hiking. The whole run on the San Juan in Utah could be done in a week, but at least one commercial outfitter takes nine days to run the Mexican Hat to Lake Powell stretch (Segment 3).

USGS MAPS: Aneth, White Mesa Village, Montezuma Creek, Bluff, Boundary Butte, Mexican Hat, Goulding, Grand Gulch, Clay Hills (15'). Baars' River Log in his *Geology of the Canyons of the San Juan River* is also useful, especially for geologic information, from Sand Island to Lake Powell, and Utah Multipurpose Map 1 (Southeastern Utah) covers the whole stretch of San Juan River in Utah.

HAZARDS: Sand waves, a few named rapids that can be tricky, isolation, bad water (carry your own).

SEASON: Anything that can run the San Juan at minimal flow levels of 530 cfs can run any month of the year though midwinter trips may be a bit cool. May and June are the best months, however, because only then do tributary streams contribute meaningful amounts of water to the reservoir release upstream.

ACCESS: For the uppermost segment (1) the primary access point lies in Colorado where U.S. 160 crosses the San Juan near Four Corners. It is roughly 25 miles to the next logical access point at Aneth on U-262, an additional 10 miles to an

The Sand Island launch area on the San Juan

access point at Montezuma Creek though U-262 follows the course of the river between Aneth and Montezuma Creek. The highway leaves the river for the estimated 20 river miles to a BLM launch site at Sand Island near Bluff. There are two accesses at Mexican Hat, one on the bend of the river east of town, the other at the northeast end of the bridge where U.S. 163 crosses the San Juan (a dirt road follows a layer of sedimentary rock right down to the river). The next access is 56 miles downriver at Clay Hill Crossing in Glen Canyon National Recreation Area.

SHUTTLE: A two-car shuttle makes a lot of sense for most of the upper San Juan, from Four Corners to Mexican Hat, though there will be long stretches for double driving. For the take-out at Clay Hill Crossing, I recommend hiring a shuttle at Valle's Trading Post or through one of the commercial river running operations in the area. It's at least 70 miles to Clay Hill Crossing from a put-in at Mexican Hat, and the pick-up service is only $25 ($50 for a deadhead, which involves two drivers and leaving a car at the take-out).

SUMMARY: The San Juan flows through relatively open country from Four Corners to the general vicinity of Bluff, much of it braided with sand islands, no rapids or riffles and plenty of interesting archeological sites (take nothing but pictures, leave nothing but footprints). A few miles below Bluff the river enters canyon country, emerging briefly near Mexican Hat, then it dives back into a thousand-foot canyon to loop through the Goosenecks and open up again only upon approaching Lake Powell.

To run the San Juan's uppermost segment in Utah, put in at the Bridge where U.S. 160 in Colorado crosses the San Juan. Since you may average only about 3 mpg on this stretch, not including stops, allow at least 8 hours to run as far as Aneth, another 3 hours to Montezuma Creek, and an additional 7 hours to the BLM boat landing at Sand Island. When you add shuttle time and any stops for meals or exploration, you will have a full day to Aneth, an even longer one to Montezuma Creek, and a good two-day run all the way to Sand Island.

The river is broad, open, flat, slow and sandy as is much of the surrounding country, but there are a few old trading posts and all kinds of ancient Indian relics. Below Aneth the country is much the same with plenty evidence of oil and gas exploration and development. Below Montezuma Creek the San Juan is less braided, and the archeological sites increase in number and quality. The broad well-vegetated river bottomlands offer excellent bird habitat. Still too low and slow for comfortable rafting, this stretch continues to be excellent for canoeing.

About three miles above Bluff a footbridge crosses the river, marking a major Indian site on the left bank, Seventeen Room Ruin. A dirt road reaches the river at the footbridge and leads toward the ruin, which is on a cliff a quarter mile south of the river. Another small cliff dwelling lies on the bench a quarter mile north of the river at roughly the same point. The San Juan to this point is infrequently floated, and those who do float it often take out at Sand Island 3 miles west of Bluff.

The BLM has established a boatramp on the right bank and a campground among the large cottonwood trees along the extensive sandy area north of the river. Sand Island makes a good landing or launching area or overnight camping spot, but it does get plenty of use. It is not a wilderness site by any means, but there are numerous petroglyphs on a rock wall on the right bank a half-mile below the boatramp but just upstream from a bridge across the San Juan (it is at this point that Baars' river log begins).

The launch area east of Mexican Hat on the San Juan

From Sand Island to Mexican Hat the river traffic increases as does the quality of the scenery. Rafts use this stretch frequently—when there is enough water—and canoeists need a bit more knowledge and skill to run this segment than they needed to run the upper San Juan. There are a few tricky rapids in the canyon. Sportyaks, kayaks and dories come into more use in this stretch, and the Indian ruins and rock art become increasingly interesting as the river enters a canyon for the first time in its run through Utah.

The river cuts a course through some interesting geological formations, Comb Ridge and Raplee Ridge, as it twists and turns in a wild series of loops and horseshoes known as entrenched meanders. Ancient Indian dwellings and rock art appear at the mouths of several side canyons—Butler Wash, Comb Wash, Chinle Wash—before the river dives into the canyon. Several rapids—8½ foot, the Ledge, Anticline—make this segment an exciting run.

So do the sand waves. Sand waves are not unique to the San Juan, but they are at their best in the shallow turbid water. They seem to be related to a condition of supersaturation of the water with silt and mud that sets up a series of waves in shallow water that build in a pattern moving upstream, "antidunes" Baars calls them. On the San Juan they may reach 8 or 10 feet in height in fast shallow turbid water. A great roaring noise accompanies the sand waves, and it is altogether a frightening experience the first time you experience them, especially if they build up to several feet in height, which they rarely do now that the San Juan is dammed in its upper reaches. There just isn't that much flow volume any more.

In the Sand Island-to-Mexican Hat segment there are Indian ruins, 6- to 8-room houses, kivas, ceramic ovens, shards, chips, arrowheads, well-preserved pictographs on a cave ceiling, great scenery and vistas through formations of multi-colored rock and exotic rock formations like the formation that gives Mexican Hat its name—the river passes right by the petrified sombrero.

From Mexican Hat to the Colorado River used to be 113 miles. Now the run to Lake Powell is only half that. For one of the best accounts of a river trip down this stretch before the dam, read Wallace Stegner's "San Juan and Glen Canyon," chapter 5 in his book *The Sound of Mountain Waters*, a delightful collection of Stegner's prose and philosophy. Clay Hill Crossing is the normal take-out now for this segment.

This may be the most picturesque segment of the river because it includes the famous Goosenecks of the San Juan in which the river loops through some 16 miles of canyon in only 4½ miles by air. It also includes some of the finest Indian ruins and rock art in the Southwest in its side canyons— fabulous country in Johns Canyon, Slickhorn Canyon and Grand gulch (see Ann Zwinger's soon-to-be-published book on the San Juan).

If you launch at the beach southeast of Mexican Hat, you will have to run a major riffle (small rapid(just around the bend, but this is a better launch site. The road down to the river on the right back at the US 163 bridge is narrow and tight but provides a put-in point below the rapid. There are riffles and rapids and high-water sand waves in this stretch, but is ideal training for sportyaks, rafts and kayaks, dories and canoes. Most rapids can be portaged or lined or cheated.

Even before drifting under the highway bridge at Mexican Hat, you will be in the canyon as the river drops rapidly but calmly into the layers of limestone. Less than two miles downstream, the river enters the Mendenhall Loop. An

The Goosenecks Overlook on the San Juan

old stone cabin that can be reached by trail from Mexican Hat or from the river, sits on the narrow ridge between the loops of the entrenched meander a thousand feet above the river.

The river flows quietly between the steep terraced walls around the Tabernacle, through the Second Narrows (the First Narrows lie in the canyon upstream from Mexican Hat) and the Goosenecks below the overlook at the state park (Goosenecks of the San Juan Reserve) into an ever-deepening canyon. The rapids begin below the Goosenecks, mostly Class II and III but a few Class IV's in high water.

For a fine view of the surrounding countryside and a good bit of off-river exercise you can climb out of the canyon on the Honaker Trail, carved out of the canyon wall by A. C. Honaker of Mancos, Colorado, near the turn of the century (some say 1894; others, 1904) at a cost of $15,000 to mine the San Juan gravel bars for gold. He took out about $1500 worth of color before he gave it up.

Below Cedar Mesa to the north, the San Juan curves its course toward Lake Powell over rapids and through deeper layers of rock: Cedar Mesa sandstone, massive redrock cliffs through which tributary canyons have been carved, each offering inviting hikes. Each is unique: most have relics of the ancient ones. All are part of the San Juan scene in Canyon Country.

The rapids—Government, False Government, Johns Canyon, False Johns, Slickhorn, Express Train (or Box Car), Grand Gulch—keep the river running exciting, but for many river runners, the side canyon hiking is the high point of the trip in this stretch: isolation from the work-a-day world and exploration of the past. There are fossils here especially in Slickhorn Canyon as well as ancient Indian Relics, especially in Grand Gulch, a network of box canyons full of ruins, pictographs and petroglyphs.

NOTE: All antiquities are protected by law: federal, state, and in many cases, Indian, which is by far more restrictive. Leave what you find where you find it so it will be there for the next visitor. These relics of the past belong to everyone and therefore to no one. Be careful of the structures, Don't climb on them, sit on them, or damage them in any way. More damage has occured during the past two decades than in the previous six hundred years. Lake Powell has drowned more sites than remain and has made many others accessible to vandalism, but that is no excuse for further vandalism. It

The San Juan below Mexican Hat

is all the more reason to protect what remains.
NOTE: From Four Corners to Montezuma Creek the San Juan flows through the Navajo Indian Reservation, to a point to keep in mind. Technically you should have permission from the Navajo Tribal Council to camp or explore any Indian lands. From Montezuma Creek to Lake Powell (actually to the confluence of the San Juan and Colorado rivers) the San Juan forms the northern boundry of the Navajo Reservation. Any camping or exploration on the south (left) bank should be done only with authorization from the Navajo Tribal Council as well.

The narrow canyon of Muddy Creek
Photo courtesy Paul Boos

Seasonal Rivers

For the adventuresome, a number of other rivers in Canyon Country may be considered runable some years or for a few brief weeks most years. While the Colorado, Green and San Juan rivers are normally considered better to run during the spring run-off, they are at least runable throughout the year, weather permitting. However, a number of streams in the area have a very limited season. They can be run *only* during the spring run-off, if at all, and that run-off season may vary greatly from year to year and some years may not exist at all.

Catching the crest of the flood, so to speak, is the epitome of success for expert kayakers and some rafters or sport-yakers, but it can be dangerous business, especially for the uninitiated. Don't try running a spring-swollen river unless you have the proper equipment and the experience to handle it, and then take every precaution. Get reliable first-hand information, not the story from a brother-in-law's cousin whose neighbor ran in back in 1937. It may be a good idea to walk the route during the dry season or to fly over the segment you plan to run during the flood season. Don't leave too much to chance or your chance of a successful float trip may be highly limited.

In the spring the water will be cold. It may be wise to wear a wet suit no matter what kind of craft you plan to use. I would not recommend an open canoe for running a high-water segment of river, especially a seasonal river that may vary so greatly from year to year. Using a dory may also be unwise, because you might end up having to carry it out or drag it along if you haven't caught the height of the flood.

Remember too that every river is a different river at different water levels. Flood-stage rivers move fast, and while many obstacles may be drowned out and easy to run, others will be more prominent. There will be more whirlpools and eddies and the eddies will be more powerful. Flood waters carry more debris and often uproot trees that may block the channel or the whole river in narrow canyons. The speed of the river will make it more difficult to maneuver—you will have less time to make decisions and less time to react to those decisions.

Further, since seasonal streams are not run as regularly as the free-flowing rivers, they are less known by river runners and there is less reliable information about them and about the roads you will need to use to get to them and to make the necessary shuttles. Scout rapids or unknown sections of the river before you run them. I know of one party that tried to run the Black Box of the San Rafael on what they though was reliable information. They had to abandon their crafts and make a hazardous climb out of the canyon.

There may be waterfalls. New rapids can be created overnight. Use good judgement and common sense before you even launch the trip and certainly while you are running it. Know about hypothermia, a subtle killer, and anticipate a night out even if you plan to make only a one-day run. Take along a flashlight and matches (waterproof) and the means of spending a night in the open if you find that the trip takes longer than you expected it to take because you had to portage too often or because you dumped and had to stop to warm up and dry out. Be prepared.

Muddy Creek

TYPE OF CRAFTS: kayaks, sportyaks, small rafts; not recommended for dories or open canoes.

MILEAGE: 15 to 20 (estimated).
TIME: one day, perhaps 1½ days; 4 to 6 hours of actual running time on the water; makes a good overnight or weekend trip.
USGS MAPS: Wild Horse (15').
OTHER MAPS: Southeastern Utah Multipurpose Map 1.
HAZARDS: Log jams in narrow canyon, isolation, flash floods, steep-walled canyon.
SEASON: from late April to early July but only a two- to three-week period during that time varying from year to year with the weather and the snowpack.
ACCESS AND SHUTTLE: Follow a dirt road off I-70 30 miles west of Green River 23 miles to a junction. Take the right-hand fork 5 miles to Tomsich Butte and Hondoo Arch for launch site; left-hand fork past uranium mine 11 miles to take-out near confluence of Salt Wash with Muddy Creek opposite Moroni Slope.
SUMMARY: This stretch of Muddy Creek flows through a steep-sided narrow canyon that usually offers better hiking than boating, but for two or three weeks in the spring, exact dates vary from year to year, it makes an exciting run, normally easy but at high water in narrow canyon there is the danger of log jams that exist 20- to 25-feet above the canyon floor (one party reported just missing one as everyone ducked to avoid the overhead jam; if the water had been a foot or two higher, it could have been disasterous).

As a hiking route, it may be damp, requiring wading, perhaps even swimming, but when the water is low, there is better walking than boating. Hikers have complained of a rash they have gotten after walking in the muddy water, perhaps from natural chemicals dissolved in the turbid water. If you try to float it at the wrong time — and only on-the-spot observation can determine the right time — you may have more walking than boating even if you plan to boat it. Several parties have had to carry out their crafts much of the way. Thus, kayaks and sportyaks are the most practical crafts.
NOTES: This canyon is scenic and rarely seen because it is so relatively inaccessible, but it does offer a different kind of experience for the expert river runner. Administered by the Bureau of Land Management, it may be known to local personnel of that federal agency. There is always a risk involved in such outings because flood-stage rivers can do mighty works. Take along spare water, spare oars and paddles,

equipment for an overnight stay if you become benighted—or get an early start—and gather all the reliable information you can from local residents, BLM personnel, and river runners who know the area.
OTHER SEGMENTS OF THE MUDDY: It has been suggested to me that a 4 or 5-day trip from I-70 to Hanksville might be run on the Muddy, but there are no campsites in the upper canyon, which is narrow and steep-sided offering no escape routes in some sections. Flash flood danger exists, and the whole area, while fascinating to say the least, is extremely isolated.

Dolores River

Largely in Colorado but with a 26-mile segment in Utah. Several stretches of the Dolores River in Colorado have become popular among river runners during the past decade. It can be run all the way from the town of Dolores near Cortez to its confluence with the Colorado near Dewey Bridge in eastern Utah, but only the lower stretch lies in Utah, about 26 miles of a 31-mile run from Gateway, Colorado.
TYPE OF CRAFTS: small raft, kayak, sportyak, open canoe with experienced paddlers (plan to portage a rapid or two), dory.
MILEAGE: 31 miles from Gateway, less from various put-ins along the dirt road downstream, but the Gateway launch site is probably best.
TIME: can be run in one day by kayak or canoe, probably a two-day run by raft or sportyak. Makes a good overnight or weekend trip.
USGS MAPS: Cisco, Coates Creek, Polar Mesa (15').
HAZARDS: Rapids in first few miles below Gateway put-in, diversion structure near Stateline, low water that means rocky channel.
SEASON: Late April through early June when the snowpack is adequate; some years it may be totally unrunable (1977, for example) due to inadequate flow.
ACCESS AND SHUTTLE: The launch site is on the left (south) bank of the river at the bridge (Colorado 141) at Gateway, Colorado. The best take-out is at Dewey Bridge a mile below the confluence of the Dolores with the Colorado though

Rafts on the Dolores River

there is a four-wheel-drive take-out a mile or so above the confluence on the left bank according to some river runners (I was unable to find it in my conventional car).

The shuttle is a long one: from Gateway to Grand Junction to Cisco to the Dewey Bridge on the road to Moab (U-128) *or* from Gateway down C-141 to Bedrock to U-46 through La Sal to US 163 to Moab, then up U-128 to the Dewey Bridge take-out. River runners in Moab can arrange for the shuttle, but it may be costly, especially if you want a car left at the landing.

SUMMARY: The Dolores flows through open ranch bottomlands to roughly the stateline between Colorado and Utah. A dirt road follows the river to the mouth of the canyon that swallows the Dolores. The current quickens, the canyon walls of red and yellow sandstone rise and black out all signs of civilization — it is a wilderness canyon for the most part. There are no rapids but plenty of good side-canyon hikes. Then the canyon opens up again to lighter-colored sandstone and signs of old mines, a ranch, an active mine where a bulldozer has worked the riverbed.

NOTES: The Dolores in Colorado has been studied for possible inclusion in the National Wild and Scenic Rivers System; at this writing (November '77) the Utah stretch of the Dolores is also being studied. A major battle seems to be developing over the proposed protective designation for the Dolores, but this writer would like to see such designation. Members of the Western River Guides Association has voted unanimously to support Wild and Scenic Rivers designation for the Dolores.

OTHER SEGMENTS OF THE DOLORES: Three other segments of the Dolores are well worth mentioning here, even though they lie in Colorado, just outside the range of this guidebook: the 47-mile Dolores-to-Slick Rock run, commonly known as the Upper Dolores Canyon, the 34-mile run from Slick Rock to Bedrock, and the 37-mile run from Bedrock to Gateway, a total of nearly 120 miles.

The upper segment is heavily wooded, flowing through ponderosa pine, pinyon and juniper forests. There are clear tributary streams and excellent campsite. The Dolores is more of a mountain stream than a desert river at this point. It has big whitewater during the spring run-off, a lot of Class II and III rapids and a real ring-tailed tooter in Snaggletooth, a Class V or VI rapid that ranks with the best the Colorado has to offer in the minds of many boatmen.

The middle segment flows initially through open ranchlands, then enters a red-wall canyon full of wildflowers in the spring. Beaver seem to like this canyon too. It is here that I found sagebrush used by beaver. Hazards in this stretch include low bridges and fences in the open areas, a few minor rapids in the canyon. At some places the canyon walls actually overhang the river, and the river is a true desert stream, turbid and slow, an ideal canoeing stream but for the minor rapids that can be lined or portaged—an expert will have no trouble with them.

The lower segment has a highway along most of its course and flows rather sluggishly through mostly-open ranchland with a short canyon at one point. It is less impressive than either of the two upper segments but pleasant nonetheless and a good stretch for fun in the boats—canoes, sportyaks, kayaks. This segment is used much less than any of the others, but is offers some nice stretches.

Escalante River

The last river in the United States to be discovered, the Escalante is by its very nature a wilderness river, and its canyons and tributary canyons are as close to what Glen Canyon was like as we have left. It lies between the Waterpocket Fold and the Kaiparowits Plateau, a desert river used more by cattle and backpackers than by river runners but a great river to run if you catch it at its peak.

TYPE OF CRAFTS: sportyak, kayak or small raft; not recommended for dory or open canoe.

MILEAGE: roughly 100 miles from U-12 between Escalante and Boulder to Lake Powell or the mouth of Coyote Gulch, which affords a possible take-out that requires an arduous climb up slickrock and deep sand.

TIME: 4 days by kayak, longer in a slower craft or if you plan to hike side canyons extensively—they are fantastic.

USGS MAPS: Escalante, Calf Creek, King Bench, Red Breaks, King Mesa (7½'), Moody Creek, The Rincon (15'), also Glen Canyon National Recreation Area map.

HAZARDS: low water, quicksand, isolation, polluted water, some fairly impressive rapids.

SEASON: late spring, May and June.

ACCESS: Put in at the bridge across the Escalante on U-12 between Escalante and Boulder; take out on Lake Powell, a long paddle on slack water or hike out sandbank above Coyote Gulch: turn up Coyote Gulch for a hundred yards or so, then climb slickrock to a bench on a left (south) side of the canyon, traverse the talus at the base of the cliff (scout before trying to carry kayaks) to dry side canyon 100 feet directly above the Escalante opposite Stevens Arch, follow up that canyon to a steep sand slope, climb the sand slope to a break in the canyon wall, which puts you on top of slickrock several hundred feet directly above the Escalante overlooking the Rincon. A mile hike across slickrock and sand takes you to the end of the four-wheel-drive road along 40-mile Ridge — it's a tough haul, but it does save paddling out on Lake Powell.

SHUTTLE: From the put-in on U-12 down the Hole-in-the-Rock Road (gravel) to the end of the road on 40-mile Ridge is a mere 51 miles, not half bad, but the shuttle to a take-out at Bullfrog Marina on Lake Powell would be some 80 miles, all but 13 of it on gravel or dirt roads (the Burr Trail) and would still require a paddle on the reservoir of nearly 60 miles, 16 down the Escalante Arm and 40 + up-the-reservoir to the wide and often windy Bullfrog Bay, a tough haul either way unless you hire a pick-up by boat on the reservoir.

SUMMARY: Another of the rivers more frequently hiked than floated, the Escalante with its tributary canyons is a wonderland of the unique land of standing rocks that made Glen Canyon — the place no one knew — so special. So well hidden was the Escalante River that Major Powell missed it during his 1869 expedition even though he drifted right past its mouth. His brother-in-law discovered it in 1872 while looking for the Dirty Devil, which Jacob Hamblin had not been able to find as a re-supply point for Powell's 1871-72 expedition. The side canyon hikes with their many arches and natural bridges make this run one of the finest in the nation — if you can catch it at the right water level. Otherwise it can be a lot of hard work on a river too shallow for a kayak. The Escalante can be hard on boat bottoms, and if you have to carry a lot, you had better have a light-weight craft.

NOTES: Probably first run by Georgie White, the famous woman river runner of the Colorado, the Escalante has probably not been floated by more than a dozen parties to date. I have talked with only three groups who have run it: Georgie used air mattresses; Nick Strickland used a small (two-man) raft, which he dragged much of the way; the Cal Giddings-Jay Dewell party used kayaks but were a week late and nearly wore out their boats on the shallow river and themselves carrying out the route up Coyote Gulch.

It can be a fun run for experts, but it could be hairy for intermediates. It is no place for novices. Scorpion Rapid at the mouth of Scorpion Gulch is full of big boulders, and some of the tight turns and narrow passages can require expert skills, expecially when the river is flowing fast and full.

The Escalante is a real wilderness river, tough to get out of once you are in it or on it. It is totally isolated most of the time even though the side canyons get a lot of back packing visitors during the spring when the river might be runable. It is only for the adventuresome and hopefully those who know how to take care of the back country. It is a land of delicate hanging gardens and awesome grottos that deserve love and respect and careful use. Tread lightly on the land wherever you go, but in the Escalante, treat it with reverence. There aren't many places like it left in the world.

Dirty Devil

A segment from the Hanksville area (confluence of the Fremont River with Muddy Creek) to the mouth of Poison Spring Canyon.

TYPE OF CRAFTS: kayak, sportyak, small raft; dories and open canoes not recommended.

MILEAGE: I had estimated 30 miles by studying the maps; the only party I know that actually ran this stretch said it was 35, but A. C. Ekker, who grew up in the area and has ridden the route on horseback, says it is closer to 70 miles. In any case, it is an estimate.

TIME: 3 days as an average, could be done in 2 by kayak under ideal conditions, 4 might be a more realistic to be safe.

USGS MAPS: Hanksville, Robbers Roost, Fiddler Butte (15').

HAZARDS: Rough water, possible obstacles, isolation, lack of reliable information.

SEASON: spring; late April through May, possible early June depending on the snowpack and the weather.

ACCESS AND SHUTTLE: U-24 near Hanksville where the highway crosses either Muddy Creek or the Fremont River, which join to form the Dirty Devil just a mile or so downstream from the bridges, or on various dirt roads in the area. The take-out is by four-wheel-drive road (trail) down Poison Spring

Canyon-North Hatch Canyon: turn off U-95 16 or 17 miles south of Hanksville on road to Doll House in Canyonlands National Park. River crossing is about 13 miles from highway, but the ford is probably closed when the river is runable. Check local conditions for washouts before committing yourself to the river. It could be a long walk out.

SUMMARY: There is probably less reliable information about this run than any other in this guidebook. It has been run by explorer scouts in high water and by BLM personnel on their own time during spring run-off, which may vary from late April to early June. The first few miles are slow, barren and dull, according to my informants, but before long the Dirty Devil enters a series of looping canyons that are joined by Robbers Roost Canyon, No Mans Canyon, Larry Canyon, Twin Corral Box Canyon, Sams Mesa Box Canyon and Happy Canyon—all flowing in from the left (east). Only Beaver Wash comes in from the right before you reach the take-out near the mouth of Poison Spring Canyon. It is wild isolated country, a land for the explorer of new river routes.

NOTES: Dr. Walter P. Cottam and Dean Brimhall walked the Dirty Devil from Poison Spring Canyon to the Colorado in the days before Lake Powell. They hauled their gear on a flotable contraption made out of a large innertube with a platform on top. They called it the Arch of the Covenant. It was upset in one riffle and the cans all lost their labels. After that they had "surprise meals" because they had no idea what was in the cans they were opening. In three days they reached Glen Canyon. They couldn't get lost, they said, since there was no way out of the canyon.

OTHER SEASONAL STREAMS: There are no doubt other streams in the area that have been run by intrepid boatmen. Parts of the Fremont above and possibly below Capitol Reef National Park are occasionally run as is the San Rafael, both above and below I-70 (the stretch above I-70 includes the infamous Black Box Canyon where boating parties have come to grief). Most of these canyons offer better hiking than floating, but if you run any of them by boat, please contact the publisher of this guidebook so we can crank the information into a revised edition.

Bibliography: ARTICLES: (recent)

Brown, J. E., "Golden Green," *Canoe*, Vol. 5, No. 3, (June 1977), pages 28-31.

Grass, Ray, "Canoeing in Utah: Barely a Ripple," *Deseret News Weekend*, August 27, 1977, page W-1.

Jaquette, David, "The Dolores River 1976," *American Whitewater*, Vol. XXII, No. 2 (Mar/Apr 1977), pages 46-52.

Huser, Verne, "Canoeing in Utah's Rafting Country," *Down River*, Vol. 4, No. 7 (September 1977), pages 20-23.

—"River Running," *Utah Magazine*, July/August 1975, pages 26-27.

—"Something's Always Happening on the River," *Western's World* (Western Airlines' in-flight magazine), May-June 1977, pages 34-37 plus.

Smallwood, David, "Tripping on the San Juan," *American Whitewater*, Vol. XXII, No. 4 (July/Aug 1977), pages 122-126.

Sumner, David, "Exploring a Desert Legend—The Dolores River," *Canoe*, Vol. 4, No. 4, (August 1976), pages 26-30.

—"Wild Rivers, Flowing Free," *National Wildlife*, Vol. 14, No. 4, (June/July 1976), pages 20-27.

—"Your Wild Rivers," *Mariah*, Vol. II, No. 3, (Fall 1977), pages 22-26 plus.

BOOKS—(general)

Abbey, Edward, *Desert Solitaire*, McGraw-Hill 1968.

—*The Monkey Wrench Gang*, Lippincott 1975.

—*The Journey Home*, Dutton 1977.

"Best of the West: Utah 1977 Package Tour and Touring Information," Utah Travel Council, section on river running, pages 62-75.

Dickerman, Pat, *Adventure Travel U.S.A.*, Adventure Guides, Inc., 1975.

Fisher, Ron and Sam Abell, *Still Waters, White Waters*, National Geographic Society, 1977.

Hogan, Elizabeth (Editor), *Rivers of the West*, Sunset 1974.

Jenkinson, Michael, *Wild Rivers of North America*, Cutton 1973.

Leopold, Aldo, *A Sand County Almanac*, Oxford University Press 1949, 1968.

McPhee, John, *The Survival of the Bark Canoe*, Farrar-Straus-Giroux 1975.

Norton, Boyd, *Rivers of the Rockies*, Rand McNally & Company, 1975.

Perrin, Alwyn T. (Editor), *The Explorers Ltd. Source Book*, Harper & Row 1973.

Staveley, Gaylord, *Broken Waters Sing*, Little, Brown and Company 1971.

Stegner, Wallace, *Beyond the Hundredth Meridian*, Houghton Mifflin 1953, Sentry Edition 1962.

— *The Sound of Mountain Waters*, Doubleday 1969.

Zwinger, Ann, *Run, River, Run*, Harper-Row 1975.

(geology)

Baars, D. L., and Molenaar, C. M., *Geology of Canyonlands and Cataract Canyon*, Four Corners Geology Society 1971.

— (Editor), *Geology of the Canyons of the San Juan River*, Four Corners Geological Society 1973.

Mutschler, Felix E., *River Runners' Guide to Canyonlands National Park and Vicinity:* With Emphasis on Geologic Features, Powell Society, Ltd. 1977.

(history and natural history)

Behle, William H. and Michael L. Perry, *Utah Birds:* Guide, Check-list and Occurance Charts, Utah Museum of Natural History, 1975.

Burt, William Henry and Richard Philip Grossenheider, *A Field Guide to the Mammals*, Houghton Mifflin, 1952, 1964.* (Peterson Field Guide Series).

Brockman, C. Frank, *Trees of North America*, Golden Press 1968.

Dellenbaugh, Frederick S., *A Canyon Voyage*, Yale University Press, (reprint) 1962 (original printed in 1908).

—The Romance of the Colorado River, Rio Grande Press, Chicago, (reprint) 1962 (original publisher G. P. Putnam's Sons in 1902)

Dodge, Natt N., "Poisonous Dwellers of the Desert," Southwest Parks and Monuments Association, Globe, AZ 1952, 1970.

Grant, Campbell, *Rock Art of the American Indian*, Promontory Press 1967.

Murie, Olaus J., *A Field Guide to Western Birds*, Houghton Mifflin, 1961.*

Peterson, Roger Tory, *A Field Guide to Western Birds*, Houghton Mifflin, 1954.*

Powell, J. W., *The Exploration of the Colorado River and Its Canyons*, Dover, 1961 (first published in 1895 as *Canyons of the Colorado*).

Preston, Richard J. Jr., *Rocky Mountain Trees*, Dover 1968.

Robbins, Chandler S., Bertel Bruun, and Herbert S. Zim., *Birds of North America*, Golden Press 1966.

Stebbins, Robert C., *A Field Guide to Western Reptiles and Amphibians*, Houghton Mifflin, 1966.*

*All part of the Peterson Field Guide Series. Other useful books in the series might be Borror and White's *A Field Guide to the Insects*, Craighead's *A Field Guide to Rocky Mountain Flowers*, Klots' *A Field Guide to the Butterflies*, Menzel's *A Field Guide to the Stars*, and Pough's *A Field Guide to Rocks and Minerals*.

(how-to books)

All-Purpose Guide to Paddling (Dean Norman, Editor), Greatlakes 1976.

Angier, Bradford, and Zack Taylor, *Introduction to Canoeing*, Stackpole 1973.

American Rivers Touring Association *River Guides' Manual*, ARTA, 1016 Jackson Street, Oakland, CA 94607 (small paperback not for sale but available to ARTA members).

Arighi, Scott and Margaret S., *Wildwater Touring*, Macmillan 1974 (does not deal with Canyon Country but has excellent sections on many aspects of river running).

Canoeing, American National Red Cross, Doubleday 1977.

Colwell, Robert, *Introduction to Water Trails in America*, Stackpole, 1973.

Davidson, James W. and John Ruggs, *The Complete Wilderness Paddler*, Knopf 1976.

Evans, G. Heberton III, *Canoe Camping*, The Wilderness Society 1977.

Farmer, Charles J., *The Digest Book of Canoes, Kayaks and Rafts*, Follett 1977.

Grumman's *Rent-a-Canoe Directory and Learn-to-Canoe Directory* available from Grumman Boats, Marathon, NY 13803.

Huser, Verne, *River Running*, Regnery (now Contemporary) 1975.

Jines, Milt, *The Kayaker's Expose*, available from 1752 Monticello Road, San Mateo, CA 94402.

Kremmer, Rick, *A Guide to Paddle Adventure*, Vanguard 1975.

McGinnis, William, *Whitewater Rafting*, Quadrangle 1975.

McNair, Robert E., *Basic River Canoeing*, Buck Ridge Ski Club, 1968.

Malo, John, Malo's *Complete Guide to Canoeing and Canoe-Camping*, Quadrangle 1969.

— Wilderness Canoeing, Collier-MacMillan 1971.

Michaelson, Mike and Keith Roy, *Canoeing*, Regnery (now Contemporary) 1976.

Norton, Boyd, *Wilderness Photography*, The Wilderness Society 1977.

Riviere, Bill, *Pole, Paddle and Portage*, Little, Brown 1969 (currently being revised).

Strung, Norman with Sam Curtis and Earl Perry, *Whitewater*, Macmillan 1976.

Urban, John T., A White Water Handbook for Canoe and Kayak, Appalachian Mountain Club, 1973.

Whitney, Peter D., *White-Water Sport*, Ronald Press, 1960.

(river conservation)

A Handbook on the Wild and Scenic Rivers Act, compiled by Jack G. Utter and John D. Schultz, School of Forestry, University of Montana, Missoula, MT 59812, 1976.

Flowing Free, The River Conservation Fund, 317 Pennsylvania Avenue, SE, Washington, DC 20003, 1977.

(U.S. Geological Survey publications)

"John Wesley Powell: Soldier, Explorer, Scientist," — 1973.

"John Wesley Powell's Exploration of the Colorado River," — 1976.

"John Wesley Powell and the Anthropology of the Canyon Country," — 1969.

(magazines)

Down River, Box 366, Mountain View, CA 94042.

Canoe, 1999 Shepard Road, St. Paul, MN 55116 (official publication of the American Canoe Association, 4260 E. Evans Ave., Denver, CO 80222)

American Whitewater, Box 321, Concord, NH 03301 (official publication of the American Whitewater Affiliation with three chapters in Utah).

Wilderness Camping, 1597 Union Street, Schenectady, NY 12309 (official publication of the United States Canoe Association).

OTHER WASATCH PUBLICATIONS

Canyon Country series:

1. Canyon Country Scenic Roads $1.95
2. Canyon Country Exploring $1.95
3. Canyon Country Hiking & Natural History $3.95
4. Canyon Country Off-Road Vehicle Trails, Island Area $2.50
5. Canyon Country Off-Road Vehicle Trail Map, Island Area $2.00
6. Canyon Country Off-Road Vehicle Trails, Arches & La Sals Areas $2.50
7. Canyon Country Off-Road Vehicle Trail Map, Arches & La Sals Areas...... $2.00
8. Canyon Country Off-Road Vehicle Trails, Canyon Rims & Needles Areas .. $2.50
9. Canyon Country Off-Road Vehicle Trail Map, Canyon Rims & Needles Areas................................... $2.00
10. Canyon Country Camping............. $1.95
11. Canyon Country Geology, for the Layman and Rockhound $3.95
12. Canyon Country Paddles.............. $2.50

Other guidebooks in the Canyon Country series are scheduled for release in the spring of 1979.

Wasatch Publishers maps and guidebooks can be purchased from retail outlets throughout canyon country or ordered directly from the publisher by mail for the prices listed, postpaid.

Wasatch Publishers, Inc.
4647 Idlewild Road
Salt Lake City, UT 84117

BACK COVER: The Colorado River with the La Sal Mountains and the Fisher Towers in the background.